The
Ephraim
Chronicles

The Ephraim Chronicles

by

Lee Nelson

ISBN: 1-55517- 465-5
v.1

Published by Council Press

Distributed by:
925 North Main, Springville, UT 84663 • 801/489-4084

CFI Publishing and
Distribution Since 1986

Cedar Fort, Incorporated
CFI Distribution • CFI Books • Council Press • Bonneville Books

Typeset by Virginia Reeder
Cover design by Adam Ford
Cover design © 2000 by Lyle Mortimer

Printed in the United States of America

To my father,
who was always there
for me,
even when I didn't know it.

Prologue

It was quite by accident that my son Russell and I found what appeared to be an abandoned wall tent, hidden in a stand of black pine. We wouldn't have found it at all if the howling wind and blowing snow hadn't forced us into the trees to seek shelter. It was the third week in October and we were hunting mule deer on Temple Peak at the headwaters of the Logan River, in northern Utah.

The timber was so thick that it was virtually impossible to see the tent from a distance of more than thirty or forty feet. I assumed it had been abandoned years earlier, perhaps by a sheepherder. The green, red and black lichens growing in circles on the canvas surface, supported my theory that the tent had been there a long time.

But then, I saw evidence that it had been used fairly recently. A short distance into the thick woods I saw a late-model generator, painted bright red, powered by a Briggs and Stratton engine, with a power cord leading to the tent.

"Anybody home?" Russell called. No response.

Pushing aside the flap, we looked inside. There

was a wood stove, still warm from an early-morning fire. The blackened chimney pipe disappeared through the top of the tent. Beside the stove was a wooden box, open on top, filled with freshly cut firewood. On the other side of the tent was another box, this one full of canned food. Behind it, was a gunny sack half full of red potatoes.

Against one wall was a fold-out canvas cot with wooden legs, a bulky, goosedown sleeping bag rolled out on top. Underneath, was a blue backpack and a green, Army-style duffel bag.

At the back of the tent we saw a folding chair and a small wooden table. On top was a late model laptop computer, the screen up, with color photos of grizzly bears passing slowly from right to left. A second table, to the right, was stacked high with papers and books.

Above the cot, hanging on the canvas wall, was a black and white photo of a beautiful young woman wearing a sheath-like satin dress and glittering high heels. A silk headband pressed her blond, curly hair close against her face. She looked like she just stepped out of the ballroom scene in the movie *Titanic*, or like she was ready to pose in an advertisement for a Model A Ford. The photo was attached to the tent surface with a short piece of silver duct tape.

Russell and I both agreed this was the most unusual hunting camp we had ever seen. In fact, after a little thought, we decided it was not a hunting camp but some kind of scholarly retreat. Perhaps a wildlife biologist was using the camp as a base for a research project. Of course, such a study couldn't be about grizzly bears because the last of these animals had disappeared from the Cache Mountains more than fifty years earlier. Perhaps a writer had escaped to this secret mountain camp to compose in total isolation.

I picked up a thick, blue, three-ring binder and opened it to a newspaper article enclosed in clear plastic. It announced the retirement of a *New York Times* editorial writer by the name of Dan Evans. The article said he had been a fixture at the *Times* for over forty years, except for leaves of absence to be a speech writer for two U.S. presidents, and to write nine books. It said he had been a war correspondent for the *Times* during World War II.

Wow, I thought, a pretty impressive guy. But what was an old man from New York City doing in the mountains above Logan, Utah, risking winter storms, deep snow and sub-zero temperatures?

Placing the binder back on the table, I reached down and wiggled the computer mouse. The moving photos of grizzly bears were replaced with a black and white manuscript page, the type style courier. There was a heading at the top of the page: "The Ephraim Chronicles."

"I think we better wait for Mr. Evans to return. He might need our help getting out of here," I said to Russell, who promptly stretched out on the cot and closed his eyes. I sat down in front of the computer, clicked the cursor into position at the front of the manuscript and began reading.

Chapter 1

Arlene Evans didn't know the biggest storm of the winter was pushing its way into Cache Valley on the morning she asked her best friend, Mabel Cowley, to leave her warm house across the street, to help start the Model T Ford.

Mabel was wrapped tightly in a brown, wool coat and wearing gloves too big for her, as she hurried across the street, her five-year-old daughter, Ella, trotting close behind, holding onto the hem of her mother's coat with both of her bare little hands. The girl's long, almost-white hair hung in curls to her shoulders. Her soft eyes were blue as the winter sky.

After sending Ella inside the Evans home where she would be warm, Mabel marched to the front of the frozen, black car and grabbed the steel crank which was inserted in the hole below the radiator. Arlene was already on the seat, having already pulled out the choke and throttle knobs.

Inside the house, little Ella, after an unsuccessful attempt to reach a plate of sugar cookies on the kitchen counter, asked Arlene's boy, Danny, to get one for her. He was six years old, and at least six inches taller.

"Your wish is my command," Danny responded cheerfully, easily reaching the plate of cookies and handing one to Ella.

"Where are you going?" Ella asked, as she munched on the crunchy sweetness.

"My grandma's house, in Wyoming," he said.

"When are you coming back?"

"Never," he said, sadly.

"Mommy said your daddy is staying here. You will be the only boy I know without a daddy. You have to come back, sometime. You can't stay away forever."

"Mother said never," the boy responded, his voice stern now, trying hard not to cry.

"Impossible. If you don't come back we can't get married."

"Children our age don't get married," he protested.

"I know, silly. We won't do it until we are old like our parents. I saw it in a dream. We were going into the temple. I was wearing a white dress. It was real."

"But if I don't come back...."

"Then, promise you'll never forget me. Cross your heart, hope to die," she begged.

"Your wish is my command," he responded, trying hard to smile.

The front door opened; the two mothers entered the house to get the children and the luggage. The engine in the Model T was purring smoothly as clouds of white smoke and steam billowed from a vibrating exhaust pipe.

After saying good-by to Mabel and Ella, Arlene helped Danny onto the frozen passenger seat of the Model T. She had already filled the tank with gasoline from metal cans she had hidden from her husband.

Since the vehicle was one of the older models that didn't have heaters, Arlene had bundled Danny in his warmest snowsuit, insulated boots, wool gloves and sheepskin cap with flaps that could be buttoned under the chin.

She avoided looking into Danny's face as she wrapped the wool Army blanket around his feet and legs. She didn't want him to see the fresh bruise above her eye, and the tears streaming down her cheeks.

Danny was a quiet, thoughtful boy, and if he did notice his mother's face, he didn't say anything. He was glad he was going on a trip with his mother, instead of having to go to school.

An hour earlier, Arlene's husband, Bill, had stormed off to the Utah Agricultural College where he taught physical education. He had been out drinking with his friends the night before, and had come home late. In anger, Arlene had protested the hour of his arrival, and the usual fight had erupted.

She was just glad Bill had wasted his gas money on beer, requiring him to walk to school, leaving the Model T for her. She would take the car, and he could have the furniture. If he didn't like that, he could hire a lawyer and explain it to a judge.

Arlene's plan was to drive to her parents' home in Evanston, where she and Danny could stay until the divorce was final. In the meantime, she planned to get a job and save enough money for her and Danny to get a place of their own. She did not leave a farewell note for Bill. Let him have something to worry about, too.

"I want Daddy to come with us," Danny pleaded as his mother threw some extra blankets behind the seat.

"No."

"I want my daddy," he whimpered.

"What?" Arlene asked, stopping what she was doing. "He gets after you every time you drop or spill something. He yells at me. He never tells you stories or plays with you." Danny didn't say anymore.

After throwing in a couple of suitcases and a lunch bag, Arlene and Danny were on their way. The Logan Canyon road to Bear Lake was the shortest and fastest way to Evanston. It was late fall, but there hadn't been enough snow to close the pass.

Arlene and Danny had been on the road nearly an hour when the wind began to blow. Dark clouds filled the sky, and even though it was midday, it seemed like night was rapidly approaching.

Arlene wasn't frightened by a little snow. The narrow tires on the Model T had good traction in up to six or eight inches of new snow. The roads were clear now, and she planned to be in the Bear Lake valley long before enough of the white stuff could settle on the road to cause any trouble. There didn't seem to be any other vehicles or the road, and she was making excellent time.

But she was wrong. The storm front entered the canyon with fury, bringing heavy snow and black clouds with it. While the wind eventually blew itself out, the snowfall was soon the heaviest Arlene had ever seen.

Trying to maintain her speed, she found the rear wheels beginning to slip on the corners. She shifted into second gear and slowed down. She found it impossible to turn the manual windshield wipers and drive at the same time. Soon the windshield was iced over, making it almost impossible for her to see the road. She shifted into first gear, rolled her window down and watched the side of the road through the opening.

Danny kept warm by hunkering down in his blanket, but Arlene began to shiver. Her thin gloves could not prevent her hands from growing numb. She felt the cold air on her bare face and legs. She wished she had worn trousers instead of her best dress. Her lips turned blue.

She knew if she stopped and rolled up the window, allowing her and Danny to huddle in the warmth of the blankets, eventually the car would run out of gas. If she stopped and turned off the engine, she probably wouldn't be able to start it again when she was ready to resume travel. Turning the steel crank frightened her. She had seen too many broken arms on people who didn't do it just right.

So she kept going, in first gear, her head partway out the open window, feeling like she was freezing to death as the snow in the road became deeper and deeper.

Earlier, she had planned to be past Bear Lake before dark. Now, she realized she wouldn't even reach the summit by dark. The snow was not letting up, and temperatures were plunging. Her teeth were chattering.

On a level spot, she stopped, set the emergency brake, and ran around the car, four or five times, in an effort to warm up. Her heart began beating faster, but her shoes filled with snow. Still, she felt a little warmer when she crawled back in the car.

"What does that sign say?" Danny asked, pointing at a wooden plaque on the right side of the car. She hadn't noticed the sign when she was running around the car.

"Temple Fork," she said.

"What does that mean?" he asked.

"It's the name of that canyon," she responded.

"Is there a temple up there?" he asked.

"No, but there used to be a sawmill. That's where the pioneers got the wood for the temple in Logan."

"Why did they come way up here to get the wood?" Danny asked.

"Probably, because this is where they found the biggest and best trees. Only the finest materials are used in building houses for the Lord," she responded, thinking finally she had satisfied the boy's curiosity. But he was not through.

"Do other things up there grow big too?" he asked.

"I've never been to the old sawmill, but I know

the sheepherders go up there, probably because the lambs grow real big."

"What about the bears? Do you think the bears up there get real big, too?"

"I would think so, but why are you curious about bears all of a sudden?"

"We talked about them in school. My teacher says some grizzly bears can stand ten feet tall."

"We don't have to worry about bears today," she said, soothingly. "It's winter, and they are sound asleep in warm dens underneath the snow, and they won't come out until spring."

"I know that. My teacher called it hibernating."

By now, Arlene realized that because her shoes had filled with snow, her feet were colder than ever, but it was too late to turn around. She thought the Bear Lake settlement was closer than Logan. She had no choice but to continue, as the precious daylight began to ebb away.

Arlene was just about to the top of the divide, when she made her fatal mistake. She felt the right front tire drop off the edge of the road. In a panic, she over-corrected, turning the steering wheel sharply to the left, and pressing the gas pedal to the floor. With the increased resistance of the sharply-turned front wheels, the back wheels began spinning, allowing the rear end of the car to slide sideways in the same direction as the freely-turning front wheel. As soon as the right rear tire slipped over the edge, the car began to roll. The motor flooded and stopped running, after the first revolution. Arlene's and Danny's screams were muffled by the deep, white snow as the Model T continued to roll.

On the third or fourth revolution, Arlene's upper body was thrust out the open window, the car crushing her neck and back before tossing her lifeless body to its snowy grave.

Now only little Danny was screaming, but he became silent, too, when his head struck the steel post separating the front and side windows. The black car continued to roll, in silence, through the deep, soft snow, eventually coming to rest in the upright position at the bottom of the canyon. The snow continued to fall, covering the Model T and the tracks and roll marks.

Chapter 2

It was dark when Danny came to his senses. He couldn't remember what had happened. He knew only that he was in a dark, cold place, and he didn't like it. He cried for his mother, but there was no answer. He began to explore with his mittened hands. He felt smooth glass and steel, and eventually the open window which had claimed his mother. He didn't have a reason to remain in the car which was half full of snow. Pushing through the white powder, he crawled out the open window.

The darkness frightened him more than the falling snow. He wanted to go home, where his mother could give him a hot bath, feed him cookies and milk, and tuck him in a warm bed under heavy blankets. But he didn't know which way to go to get home. He didn't know where Logan was. He didn't know where the road was, which led back to Logan.

He learned quickly, though, that walking uphill in deep snow is very difficult, so he started walking downhill, not knowing this took him further and further from the road, his only hope of being found.

By now, his mother's body, and the Model T,

were covered up, and more snow was falling. As Danny hiked downhill, then uphill, then down again, it didn't occur to him, that the tracks he was leaving behind would be covered forever, in fifteen or twenty minutes. He found a trail with a flat bottom where walking was easier, so he began to follow it, not realizing it was taking him further from the road.

An hour passed, then two. Danny was tired and hungry, but fear kept him moving. When the terrain became steeper and more rugged, he lost the trail. He began falling and rolling, getting up, then falling and rolling again.

He had been trudging along most of the night when he finally rolled into a deep, black hole. He didn't think the night could get any blacker, but it did. When he finally regained his footing, he was no longer standing on snow, but a bed of rocks and pine needles. He could feel warmer air against the bare skin of his face. He could smell something– a warm, moist body odor. Maybe a horse, or a dog, or a man. He couldn't tell which.

Then he heard breathing: slow, deep and methodical. The fear he had felt earlier was nothing compared to what he felt now, realizing he had slid into the den of a breathing creature, possibly one who would love to eat a little boy. Maybe a lion or bear.

Danny had no desire to find out who or what was making the breathing noise, only to get away. But he could not crawl out of the hole. The opening was too steep, the hand and footholds slippery with ice and snow. He wanted to cry, but dared not utter even a whimper.

For the next hour, in quiet desperation, Danny tried to crawl out of the hole, but without success. He was wearing holes in the ends of his mittens. His legs were rubber, his head felt like it might explode, his stomach growled. There were muscle cramps in his back, and drowsiness, like a heavy, black blanket, pressed down on him until all the fight was gone. He laid down and went to sleep, allowing the sound of his own deep breathing to mingle with that of the unknown monster.

Chapter 3

Danny was awakened by a wet, scratchy thing rubbing against his face. He could hear rapid breathing, and a high-pitched whimper. Then sharp teeth grabbed his nose. Danny screamed and began slapping and hitting at the thing. While the teeth caused pain, they did not close with enough force to draw blood. Whatever the thing was, it was not trying to hurt him. He was reminded of the time his grandfather's dog had knocked him down on the lawn. The thing attacking him, now, was no bigger than a dog. It was not a monster, but it had fur, a wet nose, sharp teeth and claws.

When Danny stopped screaming and tried to grab the thing, it whimpered and retreated into the blackness. Danny waited, wondering if he would ever be able to see again. Hunger pangs began to rumble in his stomach. He was thirsty, too. But he was not cold. It was much warmer in the black hole than outside. Plus, he was still wearing his coat, snowsuit, boots and sheepskin hat.

He didn't feel like exploring the blackness around him, so he waited for—he knew not what.

Eventually, he fell asleep for the second time.

When he awakened, he could see. Outside, the storm clouds had cleared and a bright, morning sun in a deep blue, winter sky, was shining on the den opening, allowing indirect sunlight to enter the cave.

Not more than five feet in front of him, Danny saw a huge, furry animal, on its side—a sleeping bear with its back to the far wall, its belly facing Danny. Danny could see round, wet-looking places, nipples where a cub had been sucking. Snuggled up against the soft belly, slept a yearling cub, about half Danny's size. He guessed it was the cub that had bitten his nose.

Danny remembered screaming when the cub had attacked him. Apparently, the mother had not been awakened by the noise. That was good. He vaguely remembered the conversation with his mother about bears hibernating all winter.

Danny decided now would be a good time to sneak away. With the sun shining into the opening, maybe he could figure a way to climb out. He soon learned why he had not been able to get out the night before. Moist air from the bears' breathing had condensed on the frozen rocks at the top of the tunnel, forming a sheet of slippery ice.

Danny tried once more to crawl out, but it seemed every time he achieved a handhold at the top of the tunnel, he would lose his grip and tumble back to the den floor. Two, three, four tries. He could not succeed. His grip was getting weaker. He was so thirsty, so hungry. As he sat down to ponder his situation, he shoved some snow in his mouth. The moisture from the melting snow, tasted good, but did not entirely quench his burning thirst.

He looked at the wet circles on the mother bear's furry belly, and wondered if he dared get close enough to suck out a little milk. He decided against it—too risky, maybe the mother bear would wake up and be really mad that something besides her cub was sucking on her.

But as the hours passed, Danny's thirst and hunger grew more intense. He realized it would soon be night again, and if he was going to do something, he ought to do it while he could see. Eventually, his craving for warm milk outweighed his fear of being devoured by a shaggy beast.

Quietly, Danny rolled forward on his hands and knees and crawled towards the sleeping bears. Being careful not to make the slightest sound, and trying not to touch either of the sleeping animals, Danny extended his face until his lips touched one of the firm, brown nipples. The mother bear offered no response, so as gently as possible, Danny began sucking on the nipple. The rich, warm milk flowed freely; Danny continued to suck and swallow until the flow stopped. He tried a second nipple, with similar results. His thirst and hunger at least partially satisfied, he crept back to his place by the opening and went to sleep.

Danny dreamed that another huge bear entered the den. It was the father. It licked the face of the mother, then began playing with the baby. They were a happy family, just like in the fairytale, *"Goldilocks and the Three Bears."*

But when the father saw Danny, it reared up on its hind legs, bared its fangs, and roared, ferociously. Then, while swinging its huge paws from side to side, it began walking towards Danny, who knew he was about to die.

Danny awakened in a cold sweat. The mother was sleeping peacefully. The little bear was sucking one of the nipples. Danny wondered where the father was. He hoped his nightmare was not a premonition of what was to come. He didn't know why the father bear was not with his family.

When the little bear finished feeding, it came over to play with Danny. This time they wrestled on the floor of the den. Danny had fun, too, and for a little while was able to forget his worries about what would happen if the father bear came home, or if the mother bear awakened from her deep sleep, or how he would ever find his way back to Logan.

Life fell into a pattern for Danny, sneaking drinks from the brown nipples and playing with the cub. But the cub slept almost as much as its mother, giving Danny a lot of time to himself to think about what he should do.

Every day, he checked the tunnel to see if any of the ice around the top of the hole had melted. Sometimes, on a sunny afternoon, the ice would become wet as it started to melt, but during the cold nights, the moist air from the sleeping bears allowed more ice to form. Sometimes, Danny would try again to climb out, but the result was always the same, sliding back to the floor of the den.

Then, one day, it occurred to Danny that he

might be able to negotiate his way through the icy opening if he could chip some handholds in the ice. He found just the right rock, about the size of a big carrot, sharp on one end.

While the cub was sleeping, Danny quietly chipped a handhold, then another. These allowed him to get higher in the tunnel than he had ever been before. He chipped a third hole, then a fourth. A minute later he rolled into the bright sunlight on crusty snow.

It had been so long since Danny had been in bright daylight, that it took several minutes before he could even open his eyes, but when he finally did, the view was glorious. He saw green pine trees, a cloudless blue sky, white aspens, steep mountains in every direction.

To the right of him, he could see where a dead pine tree had fallen into the split trunk of a second tree further down the hill to form a perfect *t*. He was only a little boy, but he knew the big *t* was an excellent landmark if he ever wanted to return to the bear den, perhaps to show his mother or father where he had lived with the bears.

Looking in every direction, Danny didn't know which way he should go to return to Logan. He knew only that it was late in the day, and with the sun so low in the sky, it would soon be dark. He wisely decided to wait until the next morning before beginning his journey home.

Danny could see a frozen stream in the bottom of the valley. In several places where the water was running too fast to freeze, it appeared the water was running to his left. He reasoned that since water ran downhill, it would eventually lead him to the valley where he lived. He decided to follow the stream.

The next morning, after sucking every drop of available milk from the mother bear, Danny said good-by to the frolicking cub, climbed out of the den and headed towards the stream. He made a mental note as to the location of the den in relation to the two dead trees forming the big *t*.

He noticed he was not alone on the hillside. Near the top of the hill, four deer were foraging for yellow tufts of grass. Lower on the hill, two bull elk were doing the same. The animals saw him, but showed no inclination to run away, or to attack. Concluding they would leave him alone, he continued his journey to the stream.

There was a hard crust on top of the snow which did not break under the weight of Danny's feet. Walking was easy, especially since he was going downhill. Danny hoped that by nightfall he would be home, or at least to a place where he could find people to help him.

But Danny was wrong again. Ahead of him, and to the right, a herd of deer emerged from a timbered draw. Unlike Danny, their sharp little feet were breaking through the crusty snow, making travel difficult as they leaped towards the stream in frantic desperation.

Then Danny saw the source of their fear. Three big cats, lions without manes, were bounding effortlessly after the deer. Occasionally, one of the big cats would break through the crusty surface, but for the most part, they were able to run on top of the snow, allowing them to move faster than the intended prey.

One of the smaller deer, tiring sooner than the others, began falling behind. Soon the cats were upon it, ripping, tearing, and slashing until the deer's lifeless body ceased to resist.

Danny stopped, instinctively knowing that if he moved, the chances of the lions seeing him would be greatly increased. He watched with awe as the huge cats, with blood-stained faces and paws, spat and growled at each other as they gulped down chunks of warm, red meat. Danny believed that if he made the wrong choice, he might join the hapless deer on the cat menu.

Should he remain still? Should he try to circle around the cats in the hope they would not see him as they continued to devour their breakfast? Or should he return to the safety of the bear den? If he waited too long to do something, would the cats become tired of their breakfast and be more likely to notice him?

Danny decided to make a wide circle around the cats in the hope they wouldn't notice him. Slowly at first, he began circling away from the stream, still heading down the valley, but keeping plenty of distance between him and the cats. They continued to eat, occasionally growling at each other, but showing no interest in their surroundings.

Danny increased his pace, moving uphill in a wide arc, watching the cats at all times. It almost seemed too easy. Then the ice broke beneath his right foot, making a crunching sound. Quickly, he pulled his foot out of the hole, stopping, looking at the cats. Two of them were looking back at him.

Danny didn't move. Neither did the two cats, except for their twitching tails. The third cat was still chewing on the deer.

Danny waited, motionless, for what seemed an eternity. Both of his feet were going to sleep. The two cats, who were watching him, did not look away.

Danny could not stand still any longer. He took a step without taking his eyes off the cats. Now that he had made the first move, allowing them to see what he was, they made their move, leaving the deer and gliding across the frozen snow toward the boy.

Danny spun around and raced toward the bear den, running faster than he had ever run before. He looked back only once. All three cats were coming after him. The two who had seen him were in the lead, running side by side, the other one further back. Thanks to the warmth of the winter sun, they were breaking through the crust more frequently than they had done while chasing the deer earlier in the day. Plus, they seemed more cautious, now; more uncertain. Chasing a man, even a little one, demanded more caution. Maybe the deer meat in their bellies helped slow them down, too.

Danny didn't know how close they were when he plunged headfirst into the bear den, but when he hit the floor and looked back he could see a tawny face with bared fangs and pinned back ears.

He picked up the pointed rock and prepared to defend himself. But, it was not necessary. None of the cats dared enter the den of a hibernating grizzly and her sleeping cub.

With all his might, Danny threw his rock at the den opening, striking the cat in the nose. It snarled, then retreated.

Danny turned around and breathed deeply of the musky, bear-scented air. For the first time, it smelled good to him. So good. Instead of sitting down to rest in his usual place, next to the entrance to the den, Danny dropped to his knees and rolled up against the belly of the mother bear, feeling safe and warm. A minute later, he was sound asleep.

When he awakened in the middle of the night, Danny decided it was time to give names to his new friends. He remembered when his teacher in school had talked about bears. She mentioned a famous grizzly in California. The settlers called him Old Ephraim. Since the cub was a boy, Danny decided to call him Ephraim.

It took a lot more thought to find a name for the mother. He didn't think a little girl's name, like Mary or Nancy, would be appropriate. Danny remembered his mother telling him about a great lady who had led her people into battle. Her name was... oh yes, Joan of Arc.

After deciding to call the mother bear Joan, later Joni, Danny rolled over and filled his belly with her rich, warm milk.

Chapter 4

Danny lost track of time, but eventually, he noticed that the days were getting longer, and warmer. There was no longer any ice in the den opening, and the snow outside was melting. Every day he crawled outside to watch the advancing spring.

He also noticed that Joni was rapidly losing the look of a well-fed, contented mother. And as her ribs began to show, she became a more restless sleeper. Danny knew the day of reckoning was rapidly approaching, when Joni would wake up, see the man, child in her den, and then decide what to do with him: eat him up, or affectionately lick his face.

In the end, she did neither. On a warm, spring morning, Joni simply opened her eyes, got to her feet, and sniffed the fresher air at the entrance to the den. The next thing Danny knew, she had pushed herself through the opening to the outside, where she disappeared.

Danny knew from living in the den that the mother bear had not emptied her bladder or moved her bowels in months, at least not since he had arrived. So, he figured that relieving herself was probably the first item of business following the long sleep. He feared that perhaps the second item of business would be to return to the den and check out the uninvited company.

Instead of waiting for her return, Danny decided the time had come, once again, to leave the den and follow the stream out of the mountains to Logan. Hopefully, the three cougars were not around. But he didn't know. He would have to take a chance.

When he crawled out of the den to the open hillside, he could see Joni in the bottom of the valley, feeding on the remains of a deer that apparently had been killed and left behind by the lions.

Thinking there might never be a better time to get away, Danny headed down the valley, being careful to keep plenty of distance between himself and the feeding bear. His only problem was that little Ephraim did not want to be left alone. The brown furball stayed at Danny's heels, tripping Danny at every opportunity, in an effort to play.

Realizing he was leading little Ephraim away from the safety of the den and a protecting mother, Danny decided to send his little friend home. Picking up a stick, Danny smacked Ephraim on the end of the nose, saying, "Go home. Go on, git."

Instead of running back to the den, Ephraim sat back on his haunches and howled his objections for all to hear.

A minute later Joni came crashing through the brush, full speed, roaring. Danny sat down and put his hands over his eyes, knowing his short life was about to end.

Instead of killing him, Joni rushed by, seeking an unseen enemy. When she didn't find it, she returned, still angry, swatting the bawling Ephraim, sending him rolling through the grass. Then she swatted Danny, knocking him head over heels. But the blow didn't hurt, at least not very much. While the blow sent him rolling, the sharp claws didn't touch him. Danny sat up, amazed he was still alive. Ephraim was already racing back to the den.

The next thing Danny knew, Joni had struck him again. This time he got the message, jumped to his feet and ran as fast as he could back to the den.

Joni returned to the deer where she fed for another half an hour, then returned to the den to give her wayward babies a big drink of warm milk.

Two days later, when the last of the deer had been cleaned up, Joni led her children down the valley, seeking lower, greener, warmer places where there were more things to eat. The deer, elk and moose had already moved to the lower valleys to fill up on the new spring grass. With the warmth of spring, Danny had left his snowsuit behind at the den, not realizing they were going to be gone for a very long time.

Life fell into a simple routine: Joni would nap in the middle of the day while Danny and Ephraim nursed, played and sometimes napped with her. Upon awakening, Joni would begin to feed, the cubs accompanying her.

Sometimes, she would wander into a meadow

and dig up white and brown roots and bulbs. Danny had never been very fond of raw vegetables, so he would just watch. If there were burrows in the meadow, eventually Joni would dig up a chubby rock chuck or marmot. At first, Danny didn't care for raw rodent meat, but in time he learned to pick out little pieces of flesh, always leaving the entrails and organs for Ephraim.

Danny became excited when Joni would sniff out a stash of pine nuts belonging to a family of squirrels. She would uncover the ground stashes by digging away rocks and dirt. The tree stashes had to be close enough to the ground that she could reach them standing on her hind feet. She would rip and tear at the tree until the nuts began falling to the ground. Danny could sit on the ground for hours, gorging himself on the tasty morsels.

Sometimes Joni would rip open a rotten log, exposing white and gray grubs and maggots. If Danny hesitated, the bears licked them up first. He learned to be quick, and not very fussy about what went in his mouth. Still, he did not care for the grubs unless he was very hungry.

He liked the ants much better, especially the big white eggs that reminded him of rice. The live ants had a pepper flavor which he developed a liking for, but he soon realized that one could feast at an ant hill for hours without ever getting full.

He also realized that as Ephraim grew larger, the little bear demanded a larger share of his mother's milk, leaving less for Danny, who was learning that his digestive system was not as vigorous or efficient as that of a bear. While Joni and Ephraim were getting fat, Danny was reduced to skin and bones. The only times he was not hungry was when they opened a nut cache, or when Joni brought home a freshly-killed deer fawn or elk calf. They didn't have such fare every day though, so Danny learned to fill up quickly whenever the raw meat was available.

Danny and Ephraim would usually tire of the relentless food search about the time the sun went down. They would find a soft place under a tree and go to sleep, while Joni continued to search for food by herself, eventually returning to the cubs in the middle of the night. Even though the nights in the mountains were cold, Danny was able to sleep comfortably, snuggled up to one or two warm bears. But he awakened frequently; the cravings of his digestive system hardly ever satisfied.

Chapter 5

One afternoon, while Ephraim and Danny were snacking at an ant hill, high on a steep slope above a wooded valley with a stream, Danny heard a sound that didn't belong in the mountains—a sound that reminded him of home. A bell. Clank, ding, clank.

It looked like the meadow at the bottom of the hill was filling with hundreds of giant maggots. He had never seen such a sight. Then he saw a man on a horse, and knew the man was a herder, pushing hundreds of sheep into the mountains.

A minute later Joni showed up, obviously alarmed by the arrival of the intruder. Her threatening growl demanded immediate obedience as she pushed Ephraim and Danny into the seclusion of a wooded draw.

With their feeding cut short, Danny and Ephraim were more hungry than normal when the sun finally went down. When they tried to follow Joni on the evening quest for food, she sent them scurrying back to their hiding place.

In the middle of the night, Joni finally returned, carrying a dead sheep in her mouth. Danny and Ephraim quickly filled their bellies with the rich, red meat, then slept until the sun came up. They would have slept longer but some pesky coyotes and magpies were making a terrible fuss over the remains of the sheep.

That evening, Joni again went off by herself, once again returning in the middle of the night with a freshly-killed sheep. Danny and Ephraim again gorged themselves, then slept until dawn when once again the coyotes and magpies began fighting over the scraps, but this time there were more of the hungry camp thieves. Joni decided to move to a quieter place.

That evening she brought home another sheep, and so the routine was established for the summer. Danny's gauntness disappeared, his body thriving on the rich lamb and mutton. He grew and gained weight, but no fat, thanks to the frequent wrestling matches with Ephraim who was rapidly becoming a formidable opponent with seemingly endless energy.

Years earlier, Joni had been shot at, and had once ripped off one of her toes in a trap. She had learned to take only one sheep at a time, leaving behind as little evidence as possible—sometimes a little blood, but never any of the remains. The milling sheep usually wiped out her tracks. Still, she knew better than to keep going back to the same place. There were a number of sheep herds in the Cache Mountains, so she made it a point to visit all of them, not on a regular schedule, but randomly, keeping on the move, never allowing her babies to stay in the same place more than two or three days in a row. And she never attempted to pick up a sheep in daylight—only at night. But, even that could be dangerous.

One night in mid-summer, with a full moon shining in a cloudless sky, Danny had an uneasy feeling, as Joni started down the mountain towards a meadow where a herd of sheep had bedded down. He had never felt this way before. It was a cold, confused feeling that made him worry that something bad was about to happen. He thought back over the day's activities, wondering what he might have seen or heard to trigger such feelings. He couldn't remember anything out of the ordinary.

He looked over at Ephraim, who normally would be sleeping after a long afternoon of foraging for food. But, tonight, Ephraim was not sleeping, either. The cub sat on his haunches, looking down the mountain towards the meadow where his mother was headed. Every minute or two, he would whimper his concern, sensing, too, that something was not right.

It wasn't very long after that, that Danny heard the first shot. Then a second shot. He couldn't think of anything to do but sit and wait. Ephraim snuggled closer, still looking down the hill, still whimpering from time to time.

Eventually, Joni showed up, carrying a heavy, spring lamb in her powerful jaws. But she was limping, and red-black blood was oozing from an ugly hole in her right hip.

Joni licked her wound, while Danny and Ephraim filled their bellies. While the bleeding slowed some, it would not stop. As soon as the boys were full, instead of letting them sleep, she pushed them ahead of her, higher into the mountains. The herder had seen her. In the morning at least one man—and probably some dogs—would discover her blood trail and try to follow. When that happened, she intended to be many miles ahead of them.

They were still traveling when the first morning light entered the eastern sky. Danny and Ephraim were tired and wanted to stop, but Joni pushed them forward.

It was mid-morning when they heard the dogs. At first, the yelping and barking sounded very far away, but in time it sounded closer—much closer.

A short time later, Joni pushed through some thick timber, then stopped at the base of a steep hillside, almost a cliff. She was too weak from the loss of blood to climb, but she snarled and nipped at the boys until they understood that she wanted them to climb up the steep ledges without her. They obeyed, not wanting to leave Joni behind, but knowing they were in grave danger. The howling and barking of the dogs was close now.

High in the ledges, Danny and Ephraim stopped to catch their breath. Below, they could see Joni, her back against the base of the cliff, waiting for the dogs.

The first dog charged from the woods, right into Joni. Before it could scamper away, she grabbed it by the back of the neck, crushing the vertebrae. The dog went limp as Joni tossed it to one side.

The next two dogs were more careful, darting in to nip and bite, but dodging out of the way when

Joni tried to swat or bite them.

Joni reared back on her hindquarters, her upper lip curled back to expose her white fangs, her eyes, tiny orbs of fire, roaring her challenge to all who dared fight. The dogs were careful, but persistent. The noise of the bear and the dogs was terrible, echoing off the cliff behind the bear.

Danny had not yet seen the man when he heard the first report of the rifle. Apparently, the man had decided to shoot from further back in the trees, not wanting to get too close to the raging grizzly. Joni continued to swat at the dogs as if nothing had happened. A second shot was fired, momentarily distracting one of the dogs, allowing Joni to grab it and crush its skull.

After the fourth shot was fired, Joni finally dropped to the ground and rolled over on her side, the remaining dog grabbing her bloody hindquarter, this time refusing to let go, growling and shaking its head. The man stepped from the woods, ready to fire a fifth shot, if necessary.

Danny watched, not able to take his eyes away; Ephraim huddled close, a soft whine in his chest, not sure what was happening. The cub's ears told him that something terrible was happening, but his bear eyes wouldn't allow him to see that far away.

A few minutes later, after driving away the dog, the man put down the rifle, removed his coat, and began cutting away the skin and claws on Joni's front legs in preparation for removing her hide.

Danny watched in horror until he heard the bark of the dog. It had discovered the scent left behind by Danny and Ephraim, and was coming after them.

Danny and Ephraim headed around the side of the hill, but the dog was faster, and it was just a matter of time until it caught up with them. Danny knew this, but he also knew he wanted to get as far from the man as possible before he and Ephraim had to face the dog. He was glad that only one dog was after them.

When the dog was nearly upon them, Ephraim scooted up a tree. Instead of following, Danny stepped out of the way behind another tree, hoping the dog wouldn't see him.

The dog ran right to Ephraim's tree, and began howling, the signal for its master to come and get the treed animal. Danny peeked around his tree. The dog was standing on its hind feet, its front paws on Ephraim's tree, its nose to the sky, still howling.

Danny didn't know how soon the man with the gun would be coming, but figured it wouldn't be very long. Danny picked up a stick, a little bigger than his arm, and started sneaking up behind the dog,

Danny slowly raised the stick, and was about to strike the dog on the back of the head, when it suddenly saw him. Before Danny could react, the dog had spun around to face him, baring its white fangs, a fierce snarl coming from deep in its chest.

Danny swung the stick as hard as he could. The dog grabbed it in mid-swing. Instead of hurting the dog, Danny found himself in a tug-of-war, wondering when the man would come around the hill and start shooting. Danny tried desperately to jerk the stick from the dog's mouth, worried that if he did, the dog would bite him before he could strike it.

Danny felt helpless and afraid, like all was lost. Then he noticed some movement above him, like something falling from the sky. Yes. A brown, furry ball—Ephraim—was airborne, falling from the tree, landing on the dog, driving it to the ground.

The dog let go of the stick, trying to grab Ephraim, who was ripping off its ear. Danny saw an opportunity and swung the stick with all his might, striking the dog on the side of the head. A second later, Danny and Ephraim were running up the trail, while the yelping dog hurried back to its master. The man was still skinning their mother, thinking there was no rush going after a cub that had been treed by his dog.

Chapter 6

Danny knew he was a man-child, a human being, but after watching Joni die at the hands of the herder, Danny wanted nothing to do with his own kind. He no longer hoped for the day when he could return to Logan and maybe find his parents, though he feared his mother had died when the Model T rolled down the snowy hillside.

During the first few months with the bears, Danny had remembered nothing of the accident, but in time the memories returned, little pieces at a time. He thought one day he would try to find the car. Then maybe he would know what had happened to his human mother. But he knew exactly what had happened to his bear mother, and it made him so angry he wanted to kill the herder.

But Danny had to forget his anger, at least for the present. Joni was gone, and so was the regular supply of warm milk and sheep flesh.

It was easy to find ant hills, but no matter how long they worked at it, they could never get enough eggs and insects in their bellies to satisfy an increasingly desperate hunger. Occasionally, they could dig up a rock chuck or ground squirrel, but it was so much harder for them to dig than it had been for Joni, because she was so much bigger and stronger.

Trout were spawning in the little streams in the high mountain meadows, and sometimes they could catch five or six, but it was never enough.

It was hopeless, chasing the fleet-footed deer and elk, grown sleek and strong with the plentiful supply of green grass. The fawns and calves were bigger now, and could run faster than their mothers. The berries and pine nuts were not yet ripe. And the grasshoppers were still little and too fast to catch. Danny and Ephraim were constantly turning over rocks and ripping open rotten logs in their search for grubs, but this too required a lot of strength and the ability to cover many miles.

At first, Danny and Ephraim carefully avoided the herds of sheep, guarded by dogs and men with rifles, but in time Danny began to think that if they didn't start eating better, they were going to die. Ephraim was losing weight, too. The hunger never seemed to go away, and had finally become stronger than their fear of men, dogs and even bullets.

It was a warm evening in mid-August, a half moon in a partly cloudy sky, when Danny and Ephraim went after their first sheep. Earlier, from a hilltop vantage point, they had seen the dogs follow the herder back to camp, leaving the herd unguarded.

Danny had never watched Joni take a sheep, so he wasn't sure how to go about it. He didn't know if sheep could run fast like deer and elk. If so, they would be hard to catch. But from the times when he had watched the herds of sheep from his hilltop vantage points, it didn't appear they tried to run away from things that frightened them. Rather, they seemed to find safety in numbers, in milling together in a thick mass of woolly bodies.

Not long after the light had gone out in the distant camp, Danny and Ephraim walked out of the woods and approached the sleeping sheep. The ones closest to them began to get up and move about, but they didn't run away.

Danny ran up to the closest mass of woolly bodies, grabbing one by the fleece on its back, trying to pull it away from the others, but it dug in with all four feet and pushed deeper into the herd of moving bodies. Danny bent over and grabbed a foot. This time, he was able to pull a big lamb free. Immediately, Ephraim was on its head and shoulders, wrestling it to the ground. Picking up a fist-sized rock, Danny began beating it on the head, while Ephraim chewed on its neck and throat. Soon, it was senseless, then unconscious.

As Danny began dragging the lamb away from the herd, he looked first at the distant camp to make sure no light had come on, then he looked for Ephraim who was in the middle of the herd, first on one sheep, then another; biting, pawing and growling, not really accomplishing anything other than stirring up the sheep and making a lot of noise.

Danny dropped what he was doing and waded into the herd, grabbing Ephraim by the ear and dragging him to the outside. A minute later, they were dragging their prey towards the trees, Danny pulling on one leg while walking forward, Ephraim pulling on the other, walking backwards.

When they reached the trees they could hear the distant barking of a dog, but no light came on. They dragged their victim through the timber for an hour before finally stopping, ripping it open, and filling their bellies.

Later, after the sun came up, they were high on a hill above the camp, sleeping deeply, their hunger totally satisfied for the first time in weeks.

Once again, life seemed to fall into a simple, satisfying routine. Ephraim learned to stay back while Danny caught the sheep and killed it. The approach of a lone boy didn't seem to bother the woolly creatures. Sometimes, he could grab one while it was still asleep. Once, Danny had smashed in the top of its head with a rock, trying not to draw blood, Ephraim would trot over and help the boy drag it off. Danny tried to make sure they dragged the body over grass and rocks so as not to leave a trail.

After taking two or three animals from one herd, they would leave the area and find another herd. Danny remembered Joni's last hour, fighting off the dogs, while bullets were being fired into her vulnerable flesh; he was determined to take every precaution to avoid a similar fate. Ephraim seemed to accept his leadership.

But they were not the only sheep thieves in the mountains. Sometimes, they would see the track of another bear, a track so large that even Joni's would easily fit inside it. But they never saw the bear.

Danny wondered if perhaps the track belonged to Ephraim's father. If so, he wondered if the father would recognize Ephraim if their paths crossed, and be glad to see his son. If the father was glad to see Ephraim, would he accept Danny, too, as Joni had done? It would be wonderful to have a big strong father around. Danny wished Ephraim could talk so they could discuss things like this. Sometimes, Danny talked to Ephraim, even asked him questions, but the growing cub just looked at him, never answering back in any way.

Sometimes, they would see cougar tracks, too, and Danny wondered what would happen if the cougars discovered Joni was no longer around to protect the boys. Danny began carrying a stout stick in the event it became necessary for him and Ephraim to fight for their lives.

Chapter 7

In September the nights started getting colder. Danny had outgrown his clothes, but they were rags anyway, and he wished he could find something new to wear. He had grown out of his shoes long ago, and his bare feet were tough. He could run over rocks without any pain. But, he knew when winter arrived, his feet would get very cold walking in snow. He envied Ephraim's warm coat of soft, brown fur, and would cuddle close to Ephraim while sleeping.

The bushes were covered with berries now: currents, huckleberries, thimbleberries, serviceberries, chokecherries, squawberries and even some wild strawberries. While Danny could eat half a dozen handfuls of berries and feel satisfied, Ephraim could never get enough. During the daylight hours, he consumed berries, hour after hour after hour. He ate all the time, except when he was wrestling with Danny, never seeming to get full.

But in the middle of the night, when Ephraim couldn't see the berries well enough to keep feeding, he was always willing to help Danny consume the latest sheep kill. Danny could see the results. Ephraim seemed to be getting bigger every day. He had left the hibernating den, a yearling cub. Now, he was as big as most black bears, and getting bigger every day.

Sometimes, while Ephraim was feeding, Danny would creep out on a hill or rocky point above one of the sheep camps and watch the herders and their dogs take care of the sheep. In time, he learned their patterns in moving their sheep from grazing area to grazing area to maximize the amount of deep, fresh grass in front of the gobbling mouths.

One morning, Danny watched a herder wash some clothes and lay them on bushes to dry before leaving camp with the dogs to push the sheep to a new grazing area. The time had come to get new clothes.

Danny found Ephraim in a nearby huckleberry patch. Together, they crept into the sheep camp. Worried that Ephraim might get into some kind of trouble, Danny spread a saddle blanket on the ground and poured a jar of honey onto it, figuring this would keep the cub busy, at least for a little while.

Danny quickly slipped into a pair of damp trousers and a white shirt that were hanging on a nearby bush. The clothes were too large, so he found a section of hemp rope which he slipped through the loops in the trousers to serve as a belt. After tucking in the shirt and checking Ephraim, who was still busy licking honey, Danny entered the canvas wall tent, where he realized his fondest dream.

Resting on top of a wooden box, was a hunting knife in a leather sheath. With such a knife, he could kill sheep by stabbing them through the heart instead of clubbing them to death. He could skin a sheep to make a wool blanket. He could cut off bite-size pieces to eat. He could defend himself against dogs and cougars. With the knife, he could dig out slivers and make toothpicks. Almost reverently, Danny picked up the sheath with the knife still in it and secured it to the rope around his waist.

Under a canvas cot, Danny found a pair of boots. He didn't need them, now. His feet were tough. But in the winter, when the snow was deep and he needed to go outside, he could stuff them with wool and go anywhere. He quickly slipped into the boots.

At the back of the tent, he found wooden boxes full of food, mostly canned and bottled stuff. Quickly, he opened a jar of stewed tomatoes. After popping one in his mouth, he took the rest outside and dumped them on the saddle blanket where Ephraim was finishing up the honey, hoping to keep his friend out of trouble for a few more minutes. Danny hurried back to the tent where he began filling a burlap bag with cans of sardines, peaches and beans. Slinging the heavy sack over his shoulder, he went outside to watch Ephraim finish off the tomatoes.

That's when he saw the axe buried deep in the end of a log. With such a tool, he could make short work of rotten logs where the big white grubs lived. Armed with an axe, he could stop the cougars from entering the hibernation den. He could chop holes in the ice, allowing him to catch fish in the winter.

With the axe in one hand, and the sack of groceries in the other, Danny headed down the valley, pushing Ephraim ahead of him, The reluctant bear kept looking back, surely wondering what wonderful food items they were leaving behind.

Danny made sure he made big, clear boot tracks in the middle of the trail, so the herder would think a man in boots had raided the camp, and was heading down the valley. After about half a mile, Danny stepped out of the trail onto the grass, removed the boots, tied them together with the laces, then headed straight up the nearest hill, heading for the hibernation cave where he intended to stash his new stuff—except for the knife, which he intended to keep with him always. He knew the new knife would make his life in the woods infinitely better.

Upon leaving the cave—the food, boots and axe stashed safely away—Danny slipped his hands into the pockets of his new trousers. To his surprise, the right pocket was not empty. Something very sharp pierced his finger. Carefully, Danny removed a roll of fishing line and five brass hooks.

Once he had gone fishing with his father. He knew the value of his find. He could cut a willow stick with his new knife, and fish like people did. In the winter, he could fish through the ice.

As they continued down the trail toward the nearest herd of grazing sheep, Danny marveled at the wonderful opportunities which had been made available to him in the course of only one day.

Chapter 8

In the middle of a warm, October afternoon, followed by a hoard of blood-sucking deer flies, Danny and Ephraim arrived at one of their favorite wallows in the middle of a thick stand of timber where they thought the herders never went. Immediately, Ephraim waded into the wet, black mud, rolling and churning until he was completely covered with the sticky coolness. He was content, now, and the pesky deer flies could no longer bother him.

Danny stretched out on a bed of green moss by the spring that fed the wallow, and began sharpening his knife with a smooth stone. Because he was in the shade, the flies seemed to leave him alone. Life was good. Early that morning, they had stuffed their bellies with fresh lamb, followed by a huckleberry dessert.

It wasn't long until Ephraim looked like a big, uneven ball of mud with two shiny eyes at the front end as he playfully waded back and forth through the wallow. He was having too much fun for Danny to stay out any longer. When Danny jumped in, Ephraim was upon him, playfully rolling the boy through the thick muck.

At one point, Danny felt his foot push against something hard and straight. Thinking he had touched the edge of a big rock, he didn't give it a second thought, as the wrestling match became more furious.

Suddenly, there was the muffled sound of clanking steel. Ephraim roared in pain, pushing forward, his body moving slowly because his front leg was secured to something heavy that refused to come out of the mud. The bear spun around, bawling his pain and frustration, pulling harder.

Danny crawled out of the wallow in time to see Ephraim pull a huge bear trap from the mud. The jaws were clamped tight on his right front foot. The chain that held the trap prevented him from pulling it beyond the edge of the mud hole. Danny could see where the end of the chain was attached to a log on the far side of the wallow.

When Ephraim realized he could not pull the trap any further, he sat down and sulked. He couldn't pull his foot free, and no amount of biting seemed to bother the cold steel.

·Danny stepped forward to get a closer look. All he knew about traps, he had learned watching his mother set mouse traps in the kitchen. This huge steel trap was very different, not only in size, but appearance, too.

The wallow wasn't the secret place he had thought it to be. A man had come here to set the trap, and would be back to check the trap. The man would kill Ephraim if Danny didn't figure out a way to get him free. Ephraim held still, willing to let Danny scrutinize and handle the trap.

When Danny grabbed the jaws with both hands and strained with all his might to spread them, nothing happened. He tried several times. He reasoned that a trap designed to hold a raging bear wouldn't bend before hand pressure from a small boy.

Danny sat down, examining every part on the trap, trying to figure out how it worked: the jaws, the pan, and clamps that held the jaws closed. It all made sense except for the threaded eye bolts passing through the middle of each clamp.

It took him a minute to figure out why they were there. He reasoned that the force required to spread the jaws was probably more than most men could apply with their bare hands. Plus, there would be the danger of the jaws slipping out of a man's hand and thereby crushing a hand or arm. Could there be a mechanical—perhaps a safer—way to set the trap?

Then he saw it. If the eye bolts turned in a clockwise direction, the clamps would be pulled closer together, lessening the pressure on the jaws. Danny quickly found a round stick that would serve as a handle. He pushed it through the nearest eye bolt and began turning. Five turns on one side, then five on the other. As the clamps came closer together, the jaws began to move. It was just a matter of time, now, and Ephraim would be free.

But the bear wasn't willing to wait. Feeling the looseness in the jaws, he began to fight and struggle again, pulling the trap away from Danny. The jaws scraped away hair and skin as Ephraim thrashed about in a desperate effort to free himself. Danny had no choice but to wait.

The foot began to work free, but Ephraim was pulling his foot to one side where the jaws were closer together, eventually touching at the point where they were hinged. As the paw pulled free, the two end toes slipped into the "V." Instead of pulling his toes back to the middle of the jaws where they would easily come out, Ephraim, seeing his foot free, just jerked harder. The two toes remained in the trap as the foot came free. Ephraim howled in pain, then waded back into the wallow to let the cool mud soothe his wound.

Danny just shrugged his shoulders as he walked over to the spring to wash the mud off. He worked quickly, not wanting to stay around the wallow any longer than necessary. A man with a gun would be coming to check the trap. But Ephraim wasn't ready to get out of the wallow, not just yet.

Then Danny had another idea that caused his palms to sweat, and chills to run up and down his spine. Why not? He ran over to the log where the trap chain was secured. All he had to do was unscrew a nut and bolt to get it free. This he did quickly.

With the trap free, he carried it to the beginning of a game trail that led from the wallow to the main valley below. An old boot track on the trail, told him it had been used by the man to bring the trap to the wallow. Danny grabbed a stick and scraped away soft dirt, leaves and pine needles until he had a wide, flat hole just big enough for the trap.

As he was placing the trap in the hole, Ephraim limped by, heading down the trail, wanting nothing more to do with the wallow or the steel trap. Danny hurried to finish his work.

He screwed down the eye bolts until he was able to spread the jaws and set the pan. Then, slowly and carefully he loosened the eye bolts, allowing the clamps to push hard against the jaws which remained opened. The trap was ready to catch whatever came up the trail to the wallow. After covering the trap with pine needles, Danny used his stick to scrape out a little trench, leading to the nearest tree. He laid the chain in the trench, covered it with more pine needles, then secured the end to the tree, using the same nut and bolt which had secured it to the log by the wallow.

Danny was delighted, doing to the man what the man had tried to do to Ephraim. Danny didn't figure the trap would kill the man, because he would know how to turn the eye bolts to get his foot free. But it would hurt real bad, maybe even break an ankle. So be it. Danny headed down the trail to catch up with Ephraim.

Danny hadn't gone thirty feet when he heard the roar of a bear ahead of him. Danny's first thought was that Ephraim had run into the man coming to check the trap. Danny waited to hear the report of the rifle. None came. More roaring. Then he saw Ephraim racing towards him, no longer limping.

Danny didn't know what to do because he didn't know what had frightened Ephraim. Danny did know he didn't want Ephraim running past him and getting caught in the trap again, so Danny stepped into the middle of the trail in an attempt to stop his friend.

Ephraim stopped, but didn't wait around for Danny to figure out what to do next. Even with two toes missing, Ephraim began clawing his way up the nearest tree, a tall aspen. There were no lower branches to enable Danny to climb the tree, too.

So Danny just stood in the middle of the trail, looking to see what had frightened Ephraim. He didn't have to wait long. The biggest bear he had ever seen was lumbering up the trail. Danny's first thought was that Ephraim had finally found his daddy. The new bear was lighter in color than Ephraim and Joni, and quite a bit bigger than Joni, and he was coming quickly.

Danny took a step back, still holding the stick he had used to dig the trench. With his other hand, he reached for his knife. He knew he couldn't outrun a male grizzly, and none of the nearby trees looked climbable. He took another step back. The old grizzly didn't appear to be slowing down at all. By now, Ephraim was high in his tree.

Danny wondered why Ephraim's instincts told him to run from his own father. Did father bears kill their babies like hamsters and tomcats sometimes did? Danny waved his arms and yelled, trying to look more like a man than a bear, in an attempt to frighten away the approaching grizzly. The old boy didn't slow down, not even a little. Danny took another step back, then another.

The bear was close, now, finally stopping and rearing back on his hind feet, roaring his challenge for all to hear. Ephraim roared a return challenge from his safe vantage point in the top of the tree. The big bear took a step forward, curled back his upper lip and snarled at Danny, who was beginning to think he might die.

The bear dropped back to the ground, his fangs still showing, his tiny ears pinned back, flat against his head. Forgetting the little bear who had disappeared high in the trees, the big bruin focused his attention on Danny, moving forward to catch his breakfast, as Danny retreated towards the wallow.

When the beast got close enough for Danny to smell his breath, the boy reached out and soundly swatted the bear on the end of the nose. The big bruin opened his jaws in a terrifying roar, then stopped to rub his sore nose in the dirt. He then moved forward again to catch his prey.

Carefully, Danny retreated around the hidden trap, then stopped. He yelled and swung his stick, trying to drive Ephraim's daddy away so he wouldn't step into the trap.

But the bruin wasn't about to leave such a tasty morsel, just standing in the middle of the trail. Danny watched in terrified fascination as a big paw pressed down, just short of the trap. Then, the other pressed down just beyond the trap. So far, luck was in the big fellow's favor.

Just when it looked like the hind paws were going to miss the trap, too, Danny stepped forward to swat the bear on the nose a second time. As the bear reacted to avoid the stinging blow, the left hind paw stepped on the steel pan, causing the huge jaws to clamp shut.

Roaring with rage and pain, the bruin lunged forward to grab Danny, but the boy had already moved out of reach, as the bear hit the end of the chain. The enraged animal turned and bit the trap and chain, dug up the ground with his powerful paws, jerked at the chain, but there was nothing he could do to free himself.

With all the noise, Danny knew, a man with a gun would be coming. There was no time to waste. He tried to coax Ephraim out of the tree, but the big cub would not come down, still frightened by the raging beast.

It was a good half hour before Ephraim finally began his downward descent. The big bear was sitting quietly on the trap, sulking. Danny tried to think of a safe way to free the big fellow, but couldn't come up with anything.

Ephraim was barely out of the tree, when Danny heard the first dog bark. It was too late to head down the trail. He and Ephraim disappeared into the thick timber. A minute later, a shot rang out. They knew the bear was dead.

Danny felt very sad that he had helped bring about the death of another grizzly, possibly Ephraim's father. Why had the big bear attacked his own son and the boy who was with him? He could have been their friend, helping them catch sheep or rip apart logs to get the grubs. There was plenty of room in the big den for all three of them to hibernate together. Now, the big bear was dead, and it was all so unnecessary. Danny had lost his father, then his mother. Now, Ephraim had lost a mother and father too. It seemed so sad, so senseless.

Danny began to cry—the first time since coming to the mountains. Ephraim was too busy to notice, licking the bloody stubs where the two lost toes had been.

Chapter 9

With the cool weather of fall upon them, Danny fashioned himself a sheepskin coat. By the time he made the back, both sides and two sleeves, he had used up five hides. After cutting out the individual pieces, he used the point of his knife to cut holes. Then he stitched the pieces together with thinly-cut strips of hide. He made the coat with the wool on the inside. This seemed warmer than the way the sheep did it, with the wool on the outside. In an effort to soften the hardening skin on the outside of the coat, Danny smeared sheep fat on the smooth surface, then he rubbed it vigorously with a smooth stone.

When Danny was finished, he made a matching hat with flaps that pulled down over his ears. He stuffed some extra wool into the boots he had taken from the herder. He no longer needed any of the clothing he had been wearing when the Model T rolled down the hill.

With the coming of fall, other men began coming into the mountains, some to cut down trees, but mostly hunters, wanting to shoot the deer and elk. After cooking wonderful-smelling breakfasts over huge fires, these men would wander through the mountains, shooting at the deer and elk. Sometimes, they would cut the heads off the animals they killed, leaving the meat behind. Ephraim and Danny fed on the kills, but only at night while the hunters were sleeping in their tents.

In addition to the meat left behind by the hunters, there were plenty of other things to eat this time of year. Ephraim might begin his afternoon smorgasbord by stuffing himself at a mound of half--frozen grasshoppers in a high mountain meadow. An hour or two later, he might be feasting on chokecherries by a stream, or serviceberries high on a hill. And, of course, he was always ready to help Danny finish off a fat lamb taken in the middle of the night.

Because the hunters always slept through the nights in their tents and spent the mornings wandering far and wide in search of game, mid morning was an excellent time for Danny to explore their camps.

At first, he just picked up food items he thought might help him through the winter. He carried these back to the den. Then he picked up some matches, a wool blanket, a spoon, a couple of books that he couldn't read, some rope, a bottle of catsup, and a piece of canvas.

By the time the winter storms began rolling in from the north and west, Danny was prepared for winter. And so was Ephraim. While the cub was not yet full-grown, he was as round and fat as a bear could possibly be. When the first deep snows fell,

Ephraim waddled into the den, circled around two or three times like a dog on a rug in front of a fire, finally lying down, rolling over on his side with his back against the rear wall, then sleepily, closed his eyes for a six-month nap.

Danny fashioned a canvas flap over the opening of the den which he closed on cold nights but left open on sunny afternoons. He had plenty of food, and with the new supply of matches, he intended to eat some of it warm. In addition to the food from the sheep and hunting camps, he had a large pile of pine nuts he had gathered from the pinion trees in September.

After a week, with little to do but listen to Ephraim's deep breathing, Danny found himself increasingly interested in the two books he had taken from the hunting camp. As a boy in Logan, his mother had frequently read to him. And at the time of the accident, he had been learning to read in school. He remembered stories about a boy named Dick, a girl named Jane, and a dog called Spot.

He remembered how to read simple words like "and," "but," and "go." In fact, he could read the middle two words in the titles on both of the books: "–of the." But he couldn't read the words on either side.

As he studied the letters that made up the words in the books, he took the end of a burned stick, and after much trial and error, was able to piece together the alphabet he had been required to memorize in school. He went over the alphabet again and again, trying to make the sounds associated with each letter.

A few days later, he figured out the name of the first book: *Call of the Wild*. A day later, the second title was deciphered: *Riders of the Purple Sage*. Then he figured out the names of the authors: Jack London and Zane Grey.

The title that intrigued him most was *Call of the Wild* because it sounded like what he was doing. If someone wrote a story about how Danny had lived with the bears, *Call of the Wild* would be a good title for such a story. So, that's the book he set out to read, first.

On warm afternoons, Danny crawled out of the den, book in hand, and curled up in a sunny spot at the base of the two trees that formed the big T. At first, the reading was very slow, there being so many words he didn't know. But he knew the alphabet and could try to figure out how the words sounded. Each day he determined the meaning of a few new words. And thus his vocabulary grew. He would read the same passages over and over again until he thought he had a pretty good idea what was happening in the story, even though there were still words he did not understand.

He knew the story was about a big dog named Buck who was taken from his home in California by mean men, and sent to the wilderness gold fields in Alaska to pull dog sleds. There were plenty of mean men in the story, a few good men, wolves and dogs, many with names. Reading was very time-consuming, figuring out so many new words without help, but since Danny had little else to do, he welcomed the challenge.

Danny had hated dogs since that day in the woods when Joni was killed. But while reading *Call of the Wild*, he realized that all dogs weren't bad, and thought it would be nice to have a dog like Buck, for companionship and to help kill the sheep. He started thinking about how he might take a dog from one of the herders.

Danny read *Call of the Wild* three or four times before he started on *Riders of the Purple Sage*. This book was harder to read, but in time, Danny began to figure out what was happening. The hero was trying to help a widow save her ranch from some bad Mormons who were trying to steal it.

Danny remembered that his family had gone to the Mormon Church, and so had most of his friends in school—maybe all of them. None of these people seemed bad. Then, it occurred that perhaps the herder who had killed Joni was a Mormon, too. If there were very many Mormons like him, that would explain why Zane Grey thought they were bad people. Danny read both books many times that winter, and by the time the warm winds began melting the snow, he was very familiar with the stories in both books, but there were still some words he did not understand. He was making plans to find new books as soon as the herders and hunters returned to the mountains.

When Ephraim finally awakened from his long winter nap, he wasn't very sociable. He didn't seem glad to see his friend, Danny, nor was he in any mood to wrestle and play. His only interest was food, and the few little bites he received from sharing a can of beans or peaches with Danny, didn't hold his attention very long.

Ephraim wandered through the mountain valleys, using his keen nose to sniff out the winter-killed carcasses of deer and elk. He could travel over twenty miles in a single day, leaving Danny far behind. When Ephraim found what he was looking for, he would gulp down huge hunks of flesh until he could eat no more. The terrible smells that attracted him to the dead animals, didn't take away his appetite.

Unable to keep up with Ephraim, and after getting sick trying to eat the rotting meat, Danny decided to go elsewhere for his daily nourishment. The canned food he had taken from herders and hunters was gone now, as were the pine nuts. And the herders had not yet brought the sheep back into the mountains.

So, Danny became a fisherman. The ice had melted off the beaver ponds, and there were trout swimming in all of them. During the winter, he had fashioned a fishing pole from a green willow, and after much trial and error, he had finally figured out how to tie fishhooks to the line.

Getting bait was simple because Joni had made him an expert at locating grubs and larvae under rocks and inside rotting logs. At first, Danny ate the fish raw. At least, they were better than grubs. But with the passing of time, he found himself, more often than not, using his matches to build a small cooking fire for the fish.

There were plenty of beaver ponds and fish in the stream below the den, so Danny didn't have to venture very far on his daily fishing trips. This allowed him plenty of time to study his books. With each study session he found himself increasingly ready for something new. He wished he had more books, but it would be a long time until the hunters returned to the mountains.

One day, as he was thinking about the books with pictures that his mother used to read to him, he remembered that his mother didn't own most of the books. She had borrowed them from a place she called the library. After reading the books, she would take them back. He remembered going with her to the library, a big, stone building in the middle of Logan. His mother was gone, but maybe the library was still there. He wondered if they would let a boy who lived in the mountains without parents check out books. Probably not. Besides, he thought if he attempted to go into the valley below the mountains, that the sheepherders would recognize him, and send dogs after him.

Danny decided to stay in the mountains where he knew he was safe, even though the mountains were more lonely now that Ephraim was not with him as much as before.

Even though Ephraim's jaunts covered many miles, and sometimes lasted many days, the growing, young bear always returned, perhaps only to spend a single night with Danny, then the restless bear would be on his way again. With plenty of food in his belly, the bear was more cheerful, now, than he

had been when he had first awakened from hibernation.

Chapter 10

When the first herd of sheep finally came into the mountains, Danny was sick and tired of eating fish. He watched the herd and its herder from a hilltop vantage point for several days before taking his first lamb.

The herder was new, and appeared younger than any of the herders Danny had seen before. He had a gun, two horses, and three dogs. The young man spent a lot of time hanging around camp, playing with the dogs and loafing. Danny was pleased. He would be able to take many sheep from this herd.

One day, as Danny walked to the edge of the hill to look for the herder, he saw the young man under a tree, reading a book.

Danny was beside himself with curiosity, eager to know what the young man was reading. When the herder finally saddled a horse to go check his sheep, he shoved the book in the pocket of his overalls so he could take it with him.

Danny watched the young herder, constantly for two days, during which time the young man kept the book with him at all times; under his pillow at night, and in his overalls during his travels to care for the sheep.

Finally, Danny ran out of patience. He told himself he had no reason to fear a young man who played with dogs and read books. Late that afternoon, with fishing pole in hand, Danny wandered into the sheep camp.

Looking up from his book, the young herder was plenty surprised to see a boy, all by himself, wandering into camp. The herder was not much more than a boy himself, maybe sixteen years old— skinny as a bear at the end of hibernation. He had shortly-cropped, red hair that looked like it hadn't been combed in a week, and freckles all over his face and neck. He was wearing a new pair of denim overalls, too wide and too long, with six-inch cuffs covering each ankle.

"Howdy," the herder said in a friendly voice.

"Howdy," Danny responded. It felt strange, talking to another human being for the first time in nearly a year and a half.

"Where's your daddy?" the herder asked.

"Don't have one," Danny responded.

"Then, who brought you to the mountains?"

"My mother."

"Where's she at?"

"Back at the car," Danny said, amazed he was telling the truth without giving out any important information.

"My hell, we're at the foot of Temple Peak, a good five miles from the road."

"That's why I don't have any fish," Danny

explained. "Been walking all day."

Danny couldn't believe how good it felt to carry on a conversation with someone who talked back at you. Danny talked to Ephraim a lot, but the young bear never answered.

"You'll never make it back to the road before dark," the herder warned.

"I don't mind walking at night," Danny said.

"I'll bet your ma didn't tell you there's grizzly bears in these mountains."

"No. She didn't."

"They feed at night, you know."

"If they're feeding, then maybe they won't be looking for boys like me," Danny offered.

"I don't believe your ma is waiting back at the road," the herder challenged. "I think you are a runaway."

"That's not true."

"I can't see a woman taking her little boy into mountains full of bears and cougars, and saying 'Run up to Elk Valley and have a wonderful time, my little dearie. See you in a few days.'"

"You don't know my mother," Danny responded.

"I guess I don't," the herder shrugged, indifferently.

Danny decided it was time to change the subject. He walked over to the fire and picked up the book which had been resting on a fallen log. Another Jack London title: *White Fang*.

"I would like to read this," Danny said.

"You look a little young to be reading books

without pictures."

"I've read *Call of the Wild* five times."

"I'll let you read my book if you can figure out a riddle."

"A riddle?"

"Yeah. What did the fish say when it swam into a cement wall?"

"I don't know," Danny said, after considerable thought.

"Dam," the herder said, laughing loud and long at his own joke, not seeming to notice that Danny didn't get it.

When he finally stopped laughing, he reached out to shake Danny's hand.

"I'm Tony Hunsaker, and I'll fix you some supper if you will tell me your name."

"Danny Evans."

"You start reading," Tony offered, "while I rustle up the grub." That was all the encouragement Danny needed. He sat down on the log and opened the book. He had already figured out almost all the words in *Call of the Wild*, so *White Fang* was easy, and enjoyable.

Danny didn't look up until he smelled something strangely familiar and wonderful: frying bacon. He had forgotten how good something could smell. He felt an increased amount of saliva in his mouth, and a pleasant rumble in his stomach.

A few minutes later, Danny had to put the book down when Tony handed him a tin plate heaped high with fried potatoes and onions and three thick strips of bacon. Bright red catsup had been poured over the potatoes. Danny also realized he had forgotten how good something could taste—better even than raw mutton. Danny started picking up the food with his fingers and shoving it in his mouth.

"Would you like to use my spoon?" Tony asked.

Danny's mouth was too full to answer. He just shook his head. He didn't need a spoon to slow him down.

"How come your hair is so long?" Tony asked. "You look like a girl."

Danny stopped chewing. He had never even thought about his hair being long. Of course it would be long. He hadn't attempted to trim it since coming to the mountains. He started chewing again, not bothering to answer the question. Tony didn't mind. He just seemed glad to have someone to talk to. A sheep camp is a lonely place, even with three dogs and five hundred sheep.

"Won't have to worry about the grizzlies much longer," Tony said in an effort to keep the conversation going.

"Why not?" Danny mumbled, his mouth full of potatoes.

"The Association hired Frank Clark from Malad to catch'm all. They say he's killed a hundred bears. Might take a year or two, but he'll get'm, every last one."

"How does he catch them?" Danny asked, feeling like a spy in an enemy camp.

"He baits them in, then shoots or traps them."

"What kind of bait does he use?" Danny asked.

"The best there is. Live sheep. Brings a whole

herd with him. If a bear's got a taste for lamb or mutton, it's just a matter of time until Frank gets 'm. Frank Clark always gets his bear."

Danny started to shiver, feeling cold sweat on his back and neck. "What does this Frank Clark look like?" Danny asked.

Before Tony could answer, all three dogs started barking. Two, were running towards the nearby sheep herd, while the third ran behind Tony, like it was seeking protection. It continued to bark. The sun had disappeared behind the western hills a few minutes earlier, but there was still plenty of light to allow the two boys to see what was happening.

Danny dropped his plate and jumped up on the log he had been sitting on to get a better look. He and Tony saw the cause of the commotion at the same time.

Ephraim was in the middle of the herd of sheep, growling with delight, biting and swatting the helpless woolly creatures, slinging them in every direction, killing some outright, maiming and wounding others. It was as if Ephraim was having so much fun, he just couldn't bring himself to stop. He had already killed more than he could eat in a week.

Tony ran to the nearest tree and grabbed his rifle, a lever-action Winchester, pumped a cartridge into the chamber, and raised the rifle to his shoulder. He had just gotten the bear in his sights and was squeezing the trigger, when a little hand pushed the barrel to one side. The gun went off; the bullet missed its intended target by a mile.

"Get away, you little brat," Tony hissed, all the

friendliness gone from his voice. But the damage had been done. Upon hearing the report of a rifle, Ephraim forgot about the fun he was having, waded out of the sheep herd and was bounding toward the nearest timber, the two dogs nipping at his heels. Before Tony could pump another cartridge into the chamber and take aim a second time, Ephraim had disappeared into the woods.

A few seconds later, the barking from one of the dogs, ended with a single yelp. Then all was quiet. A few moments after that, the second dog emerged from the woods, running as fast as it could, back to camp.

"That dog killer won't get away this time," Tony said to himself in a soft voice, almost a whisper. "Can't go after him at night, but come morning...." He released the hammer on the rifle to the safety position, turning to say something to Danny.

But Danny was gone, and so was the book. Tony scratched his head. No boy he had ever known would run off into the night, in the woods, especially after seeing a grizzly bear. No boy he had ever known would steal a book, when the library in town would give you all the books you could read in ten lifetimes, for free.

Chapter 11

After making sure the shooting had sufficiently frightened Ephraim, to drive him far enough away that Tony would never catch up, Danny returned to the den to devour the new book. Tony had been so nice to him before trying to shoot Ephraim, that Danny decided he would return the book to Tony as soon as he had read it a few times.

As he pondered the events of the previous evening, remembering the alarm he had felt when Tony aimed the rifle to shoot, Danny realized what a blessing it had been that Ephraim had picked that particular evening to wade into Tony's herd. The bear was getting careless, forgetting the lesson learned from his mother, that sheep should be taken only under cover of darkness. Thanks to Danny, the bullet had missed its mark. As a result of this near-miss, hopefully, in the future, Ephraim would take sheep only at night.

And Ephraim did just that. In time, he learned to hunt and travel exclusively at night, when he was safe from the white man's guns. Also, he never forgot the afternoon at the wallow when he had lost two toes in the steel trap—the same trap that had caused his father's death. He was continually alert for more traps, not just in wallows, but also along well-used trails, and around any dead animal he had not killed himself. Every time Ephraim found a trap, he would flip it to one side, sometimes setting it off, sometimes not. Such findings made him only more cautious.

As Ephraim grew larger, stronger, and faster, he became less interested in the menu items that didn't fill him up, like grubs, ants and ground squirrels. But this didn't mean he ate more sheep. He found it increasingly easy to catch an occasional deer or elk, which he could put down with a single blow from one of his powerful paws. Also, the cattle the herders were bringing to the mountains were easy prey. Lots of good things to eat, and life seemed safe from the white man's guns, if he hunted only at night.

But, as his ability to fill his belly increased, Ephraim seemed more and more content to live by himself. He didn't need Danny to help get food, nor did he seem to need Danny's companionship. So the two spent less and less time together, except during the hibernation months when both occupied the same den. Danny liked snuggling next to a huge, warm bear on cold winter nights. He found comfort in the sound of Ephraim's deep breathing. It was easy to keep the den warm and clean during the winter months because the bear's bowels and urinary tract were dormant during hibernation.

Danny improved, too, in his ability to get food, especially after he picked up a Winchester rifle and two boxes of ammunition from a vacated hunting camp. Now, he had all the meat he wanted during the long winter months. That, combined with an occasional jar of peaches or applesauce from a hunting camp, made him comfortable. Occasionally, he got lucky and found another book, eventually building his library to nearly twenty books.

Occasionally, when life became routine or boring, Danny would enter a sheep or cow camp where he would strike up a conversation with the herders, sometimes sharing a meal or two, being careful not to reveal anything that might put himself or Ephraim at risk.

Sometimes he would climb to the top of one of the peaks to the west and look into the valley where the people lived, wondering how life would be different, down there. He wasn't sure why he was afraid to go back to the place where he had lived as a little boy. He guessed his mother had been killed in the car accident, but somewhere down there lived his father—the man his mother had decided to leave behind, but still his father. He didn't know why he had felt so bad when Ephraim's father had been killed, or why he longed for a father of his own. He just knew it was something he wanted, like Ephraim wanted to hibernate when the heavy snow came in the fall.

Months became years. Danny grew to his full size, which wasn't a fourth as big as Ephraim. Years passed until Danny couldn't remember exactly how long he had been in the mountains, only that it had seemed a lifetime.

The rigorous outdoor living, combined with the high-protein diet, allowed his body to become muscular and athletic. His energy seemed endless. It felt good to climb the highest mountain, or spend hours chopping a hole in a beaver dam so he could let the water out, thereby trapping the fish in shallow pools where they were easier to catch. Sometimes, Ephraim would sit on the bank, watching until the water was shallow enough to wade in with Danny, to gobble up the fish.

Danny had learned to live in relative comfort and safety, but something was missing. Even with all the books, he sometimes felt so lonely he could hardly stand it. There were new stirrings and surges of warmth in his young body that he didn't understand, that caused an increasing longing for-he knew not what.

He reasoned that he had taken so many sheep and other items from the herders and hunters that if they ever got their hands on him, they would lock him in jail, or maybe kill him. He was sure the consequences would be severe, so he stayed by himself, in spite of the yearnings.

But with his frustrations, came carelessness. One fall afternoon Danny stayed too long in a hunting camp. Just as he was picking up his burlap bag filled with cans of pears and sardines, two hunters stepped from the woods, both holding rifles aimed at Danny. He dropped the bag of stolen goods.

"I was just..." Danny started to say, before one of the men cut him off.

"Don't tell me any lies, Camp Robber," one of

the men said in a gruff voice. "We know what you was doin. But you did it in the wrong camp. We're the law." The largest of the two men, who had a big, bushy, brown mustache on his well-fed face, removed a hand from his rifle, and pulled back one side of the front of his coat, revealing a huge, shiny badge.

"You're under arrest, Camp Robber," the officer continued. "And don't even think about running. We will shoot, and both of us are crack shots."

"My name isn't Camp Robber," Danny objected.

"I'll bet it is," the officer argued. "We've got a file with your name on it so thick, a man can hardly pick it up without stuff falling out. I know what foods you like:—peaches, applesauce, sardines, too. You take matches and bullets, but never money. Now turn around and put your hands behind your back."

Danny obeyed, and before he had a chance to think about what was happening, he felt the cold steel of handcuffs on his wrists.

"What are you going to do with me?" Danny asked.

"Feed you supper, bed you down for the night, then take you to jail."

Danny's worst fears were realized. He was going to jail. He didn't know if he would stay there for the rest of his life, or if they would take him out and hang him. Somewhere in the back of his mind, he vaguely remembered that in Utah criminals were hanged. Over the years, he had taken so much stuff...surely they would hang him.

The next morning, Danny found himself on a horse, his hands still handcuffed behind his back, heading out of the mountains and back to civilization.

They were about halfway down the right hand fork of the Logan River when they came upon a herd of sheep heading in the opposite direction.

"I'll be damned, if it ain't Frank Clark," the big deputy said. "Best bear killer in the west, and he's bringing a whole herd of bait with him."

Clark was a strong-looking man with fierce, piercing eyes, and a weathered look from spending long periods of time in the mountains. Around his neck he wore a necklace consisting of several dozen black bear claws. He was leading three pack horses carrying his camp supplies. A little dog was following his horse while others were helping herd the sheep. On top of one of the packs, was a huge bear trap, larger than the one that had caught Ephraim's father.

The deputies stopped and chatted with Clark for a few minutes. "You won't have to worry about your stuff being stolen," one of the deputies explained, pointing over at Danny, whose hands were still handcuffed behind his back. "We caught the Camp Robber."

"Seen any bear sign?" Clark asked, not seeming very interested in the camp thief.

"Every herder is losing sheep," the deputy explained. "Might be several bears, or just one that's real hungry. Must be grizzly, by the size of the tracks."

"Good. I like to catch the big ones," Clark said, ending the conversation. He clucked to his horse, continuing his journey up the canyon.

Danny wished he could get away so he could find Ephraim. But even if he could, there would be no way to communicate to a hairy beast the seriousness of this new threat. Ephraim would have to figure it out by himself—hopefully before Frank Clark could catch and kill him. Danny felt very sad and helpless as the horses continued down the trail.

Chapter 12

Life in jail was much better than Danny thought it might be. They didn't beat him, or starve him, or deprive him of anything he needed. They kept him in a clean cage with a toilet and a bunk more comfortable than any place he had slept, in the mountains. Best of all, they brought him three meals a day–hot, good food with tastes he thought he had forgotten.

At first they didn't believe Danny when he told them he lived in the mountains. They didn't believe him either, when he said his name was Danny Evans, because they could find no record of such a boy in Cache Valley, and no boy by that name had been reported missing. When he told them the names of his parents, they could find no matches for those names either, so again they doubted he was telling the truth.

Danny kept waiting for the authorities to punish him for his crimes. The worst thing they did to him was take his clothes and force him to take a shower, with soap. He actually enjoyed the experience. Afterwards, they gave him clean clothes, and cut his hair shorter than it had ever been.

But, by far, the best thing that happened, was a visit on the third day by an elderly lady who said she was a librarian. She asked Danny if he would like to read a book.

"Sure," he said, doubting her sincerity. He told her his favorite authors were Jack London and Zane Grey. An hour later she returned with six books for him, three from each author. He could hardly believe his good fortune. Had he known they were going to treat him like this, he would have turned himself in, years ago. Now that he had books to read, he was content to spend at least the remainder of the winter in jail.

But that wasn't to be. After about ten days, the two deputies who had arrested Danny, put him in handcuffs again and took him to see the judge.

After the judge explained the court's quandary in deciding what to do with the boy, the judge surprised everyone by asking Danny what he wanted to do.

The deputy with the mustache was about to object, when Danny answered the question.

"I'd like to stay in jail until I've read all the books in the library. Then, in the spring, go back to the mountains."

"Neither of those alternatives is acceptable," the judge responded.

"Why not?" Danny asked, his confidence growing, getting the feeling the judge was his friend who didn't like the two officers any more than he did.

"I can't keep a minor in jail for taking three

cans of pears, a jar of applesauce, and some sardines. And I can't send a boy into the mountains, alone, to live by himself."

"I could stay with my big brother," Danny suggested.

"You didn't tell us you had a brother," one of the officers blurted out, without permission.

"Finally, we are getting somewhere," the judge said, motioning the officer to silence.

"What is your brother's name?" the judge asked.

"Ephraim," Danny responded.

"Ephraim what? What's his last name?"

Danny had to think a minute. Ephraim didn't have a last name, but he didn't want to tell the judge that.

"His name is Ephraim, Ephraim Bear," Danny offered.

"And where does Mr. Bear live?" the judge asked.

"I don't know the address, but his house is in the mountains. He travels a lot in the summer. He's in the food business. But he's home in the winter. That's when I stay with him."

"Why hasn't he come in to claim you, or to get you out of jail?" the judge asked.

"He has a little trouble getting up in the morning, this time of year," Danny responded, surprised at his own cleverness. "Besides, he doesn't know I'm here."

"Would you tell the officers how to find Mr. Bear, so he can come and get you?" the judge asked.

"I wouldn't do that, sir," Danny responded. "If you let me go, I could find him, but I can't tell the officers how to find him."

"And why not?"

"I fear for his safety," Danny responded, honestly.

"Is he in some kind of trouble?" the judge asked.

"He has been known to take a few sheep without paying for them," Danny responded, pleased he was still telling the truth, but not sure he was doing himself any good.

"I suppose we are back to first base," the judge reasoned, thoughtfully. "We can't release the boy into the custody of a rustler. So I suppose we'll have to find a foster home, but who will want a wild boy from the mountains? A thief, to boot, who keeps company with rustlers."

"How about old man Nibley?" the deputy asked.

"You mean Dr. Stirling Nibley, the bachelor professor?"

"That's the one. Likes problem boys. Nobody gets the best of him."

"But he's an atheist, and doesn't have a wife," the judge objected.

"His housekeeper can do the mother stuff," the deputy argued. "As for the atheism, our little camp thief doesn't appear to be a missionary prospect, anyway."

"And if the professor doesn't want him?" the judge asked.

"He'll want him, all right, when you tell him about all the books the kid is reading," the deputy argued. "Tell Nibley this kid has more passion for books than any student at the college."

"Take the boy back to jail until I've had a chance to chat with Dr. Nibley," the judge said, ending the meeting.

Two days later, Danny was released into the custody of Professor Stirling Nibley. Before leaving the jail, the deputy warned Danny that if he tried to run away from the professor, the law would find him, and next time he would stay in jail a lot longer. Danny doubted that the deputies could find the den he shared with Ephraim, but, still, he didn't want them looking for him. They might get lucky, and if they did, Ephraim might have to pay a terrible price.

Even before he met the professor, Danny decided not to do anything in a hurry. Besides, it might be interesting living with the professor, at least during the winter months.

Chapter 13

"To mix our observations with childish notions of magic, fantasy, and religion, is to cripple our perception of the world around us," Professor Nibley explained as he and Danny sat in his study, waiting for the housekeeper and cook, Rita, to call them to supper.

The professor was an older man, very thin and somewhat tall. He had a neatly-trimmed beard brown with white and black hairs, causing a salt and peppery look. There was closely-cropped hair on the back part of his head, but none on the front. But unlike most balding men, he made no effort to cover up the bare places by combing over hair from the other places.

Danny had never seen such a room. The ceiling was higher than Ephraim could reach, standing on his hind feet. Every inch of wall space, except for a single window and door, was covered with books on wooden shelves. Danny didn't know if the public library had this many books.

Danny wasn't sure what the professor was talking about, but listened politely. He was glad to be out of jail. He was free now, to stay with the professor, or go to the mountains as circumstances required. Danny felt better knowing he had choices.

"Did you find God in the mountains?" the professor asked.

"What?" Danny responded.

"Is God in those mountains? When Moses went up on the mountain he said God spoke to him through a burning bush. Joseph Smith said when he went into the woods, God spoke to him. You lived alone in the mountains. Did you find God?"

"No," Danny responded, simply.

"What did you find?"

"Bears, deer, elk, lots of sheep, snow in the winter and green grass in the summer."

"I didn't find him in any of these books, either," the professor confessed. "And I have read them all, some several times." Danny looked around the room one more time, marveling at all the beautiful books.

"There seems to be a tendency in most people to get silly from time to time," the professor continued. "Sometimes, the condition becomes permanent. In all the recorded histories of every culture in the history of the world, we see absurd beliefs, practices, theories, and attitudes that are utterly ridiculous. Do you understand what I'm saying?"

"No, sir."

"Jonah didn't live in the belly of a fish. Moses didn't part the Red Sea with a stick, and Jesus didn't walk on water, unless it was frozen after a particularly cold night."

"In India, they have transcendental meditation," the professor continued. "People pay money to learn to fly. Instead, the foolish students look like giant frogs trying to jump. Nobody really flies, believe me."

"There's a fountain in France where people bring sick children, believing a dip in the holy water will make the patient well.

"In ancient China, there are recorded sightings of flying, fire-spitting dragons. Today, we have UFOs. The newspapers report how a lonely woman is dragged by aliens into their spaceship where they look up her dress and are so frightened by what they see that they flee to Alpha Centuri.

"In the Philippines, sick Americans pay magicians to pull handfuls of chicken guts from their bodies. In America, we have chiropractors and homeopaths who can charge more money if they wear white smocks, and even more if they have machines with flashing lights that make buzzing sounds.

"It all started ten thousand years ago when a trader in northern Egypt learned how to predict the spring runoff in the Nile River by measuring the snow depth in certain mountains. Instead of telling everyone about his findings, he told farmers and politicians, if they would pay him to perform certain rituals, the river would bring more water for the crops. Thus was born the first priesthood. What do you think, Danny?"

"I don't know about any of these things," Danny responded, "except maybe Santa Claus."

"Don't tell me you believe in Santa."

"He never brought me any toys when I was living in the mountains," Danny said. "So I guess I don't believe in him. My mother used to pray with me, and tell me about God, but that was a long time ago."

"I don't believe in God for the same reasons I don't believe in Santa Claus, Mother Goose or Bigfoot," the professor said, as Rita, a plump, middle-aged woman wearing a white apron, announced supper was ready. Danny followed the professor into the dining room.

Danny was pleased with all the good things on the table: bottled peaches, a saucer full of pickles, boiled eggs, freshly-sliced bread with butter, honey and purple jam, sliced cheese, and a pitcher of milk.

"Do you believe in science?" the professor asked, as they seated themselves at the table.

"I don't know what it means to believe in science," Danny responded.

"Science is simply a logical process of discovering the truth in the world around us. The illusion is that science is a set of strange rules, a religion that speaks algebra. It is not."

Danny wished the professor would stop talking so they could eat. It was not to be.

"I would like to offer a scientific blessing on the food," the professor said, folding his arms and closing his eyes. Danny didn't know what to think— a godless man wanting to say a blessing on the food. Danny closed his eyes, folded his arms, and waited.

"If there be a God in heaven," the professor began, "I thank you for this food, even though I bought it with my own money. In addition to blessing it so we won't be poisoned, I ask thee to validate the prayer of a scientist, and rekindle the faith of an agnostic by turning these eggs into T-bone steaks, and this milk into wine. Amen."

With his eyes still closed, the professor reached out over the table and asked Danny to pass him the T-bone steaks. Danny handed him the bowl of eggs. It wasn't until the professor had shoved one in his mouth that he finally opened his eyes,

"So what are you thinking?" the professor asked.

"That I'm hungry, and wish I could start eating," Danny responded, preferring to chew on real food rather than philosophical subjects.

"First, tell me what we learned from our little experiment with prayer," the professor said, while chewing his egg.

"That there's no God?" Danny responded, hoping to please the professor with an answer that would end the discussion.

"That's one possibility. Give me another."

"Maybe God didn't answer your prayer because he doesn't like you," Danny said, thoughtfully.

"Excellent, excellent. Now you're beginning to sound like a scientist. What's another possibility?"

"Maybe, a million people were praying at the same time you were blessing the food. And maybe some of them were praying for stuff much more important than changing eggs to steak. So, maybe your blessing wasn't important enough to get God's attention. Maybe, he didn't even hear you."

"Excellent answer. Let's eat," the professor said, finally motioning for Danny to help himself to the food.

After supper, Danny followed the professor back to the study. Danny waited quietly, while the old man removed two books from the shelves. After wiping away the dust, he handed them to Danny, who needed a little help reading the titles.

The first volume was *Origin of the Species* by Charles Darwin. The second, was *The Adventures of Huckleberry Finn* by Mark Twain.

The professor told Danny to begin reading both books the next day. After he had read each volume twice, he would be given more books to read. In the evenings they would discuss the things he had read, plus the professor would teach him the multiplication tables and simple division. If Danny worked hard and mastered his studies, in a few weeks he would be allowed to attend public high school with other young people his own age.

While Danny looked forward to reading the books, even learning arithmetic, he didn't want to go to school. Just the thought of doing that, frightened him, made him feel sick to his stomach, and he didn't know why.

Chapter 14

Danny's life fell into a comfortable routine. Every morning after breakfast with the professor, Danny retired to the study where he curled up in a huge over-stuffed chair to read. After reading *Origin of the Species* and *The Adventures of Huckleberry Finn* twice, he found more titles by Zane Grey and Jack London.

Then one evening, the professor brought home a new book he had picked up at a local bookstore: *Tarzan of the Apes*, by Edgar Rice Burroughs. It was by far the most difficult of anything Danny had read: longer sentences and many more words he didn't know. But the professor had showed him how to use the dictionary, explaining that with Webster at his side, he could now read anything.

Danny stayed up all night, struggling through the first nine chapters. In some sentences, he would have to look up three or four words, and re-read the sentence four or five times before he understood. But the hard work didn't matter. This was his story, in Africa: a boy raised by the giant apes after his parents had died.

Danny couldn't sleep, driven to see how Tarzan

survived, a lone boy among the wild animals in the wilderness.

The next morning, when the professor saw Danny's disheveled hair and bloodshot eyes, realizing the boy had stayed up the entire night, the old man laughed with delight, brought the boy a plate of breakfast food, and headed off to school, leaving Danny alone to continue his quest until fatigue forced him to stop.

Occasionally, when his neck ached and his eyes felt like they might burst, Danny would get up from the chair and walk around the room, the book in his hands as he continued to read. Several times during the course of the day, he took short naps, but never for more than ten or fifteen minutes. Sometime in the middle of the second night, he finished. Holding the book close against his chest, he stretched out on the floor and fell into a deep sleep, dreaming of the jungle boy who had not only survived, but prospered in the land of the giant apes.

The next morning, instead of waking the boy for breakfast, the proud professor gently placed a wool blanket over his sleeping wonder. That night, the professor brought home a second Tarzan volume which was consumed almost as quickly as the first.

When Danny needed a break from his reading, he looked at a paper the professor had given him, listing jobs that needed to be accomplished outside. Danny raked leaves, dug potatoes, painted fences, and trimmed trees. He worked hard and fast, enjoying the strength that surged through his young muscles. It felt good to get out of breath and feel the cool sweat on his face and back.

Sometimes, Danny walked to the market with Rita and carried the groceries home for her. Late one afternoon while they were inside the store, Rita asked Danny to go back to the meat counter and get a leg of lamb. Danny didn't think about what he was doing until the butcher slapped the raw hunk of flesh down on a brown piece of butcher paper, directly in front of Danny. As he looked at the raw sheep flesh, his mouth began to water, and he found himself longing to go hunting again with Ephraim.

Walking back to the front of the store, Danny stopped, hesitated, then carefully unwrapped one end of the leg of lamb. When he didn't think anyone was watching, he bit off a chunk of raw flesh. He couldn't believe how good it tasted, bringing back a rush of memories involving hunting, killing and feasting. He ripped off another chunk of flesh, then another.

Suddenly, while his face was buried in the leg of raw lamb, chewing off another bite, Danny became aware that someone was watching. He had been so engrossed in eating, that he hadn't seen anyone approach, but he could sense a presence, feel eyes looking at him.

Danny jerked his head up, not thinking to wipe away the smeared blood on his mouth and cheeks, and found himself looking into the deepest blue eyes he had ever seen. They belonged to a young woman who was standing not ten feet away, a look of surprise and confusion on her pretty face. There was plenty of curl in the golden hair that barely touched the top of her shoulders. She was wearing a gray dress, just tight enough to hint of the perfect figure underneath,

Danny couldn't think. The blood rushed to his head, and his heart pounded. Instead of blushing, or looking away, or apologizing like a civilized boy ought to, Danny responded by instinct, after the fashion of his hairy friends of the forest.

Continuing to look directly at the beautiful face, his eyes narrowed to blazing orbs. Without realizing what he was doing, Danny curled back his upper lip as a deep, guttural growl emerged from the depths of his chest.

Placing a hand over her mouth, the girl began to back up, then turned and disappeared beyond the end of the isle. Quickly, Danny re-wrapped the leg in the brown paper and hurried to find Rita. He felt stupid, awkward, embarrassed. He decided that from now on, Rita would have to get groceries by herself. He would stay home in the safety of the professor's yard.

But, whenever he thought of the girl who had caught him chewing on the raw leg of lamb, a warm, comfortable feeling fell over him, like a wool blanket on a cold night. It was a warm confident feeling, the exact opposite of the cold, confusing feeling, he had felt the night Joni was shot.

That evening, Danny made more mistakes than usual as the professor quizzed him on his timestables and long division, and when he curled up in his usual place to read, he found himself staring at black ink on white paper. The ideas and thoughts on the printed pages could not enter his mind, because it was filled with a picture of a young woman with thick yellow hair, staring at him, hand over mouth, frightened, backing away. Even though Danny had left the market, hours earlier, his heart was still pounding. He didn't understand.

"I see, you haven't turned a page in nearly an hour," the professor observed. "Is something wrong?"

"In the market, today," Danny began to explain, with more hesitation than usual in picking his words, "a girl caught me eating some raw lamb."

The professor began to laugh. "Did you tell her that's how the bears eat?"

"It wasn't funny. I had blood on my face. I growled at her. She was frightened and ran away. It was awful."

The professor continued to laugh, then asked if the girl was pretty.

"Yes," Danny said.

"That makes the matter less funny, but still, you will get over it."

"I want to go back to the mountains," Danny said, looking directly into the professor's face.

"What?" All the mirth had disappeared. The professor was as serious as Danny now.

"I don't belong here. I want to go back. I will still read, if you will lend me books."

Without responding, the professor began pacing back and forth, looking first at the ceiling, then at the floor, his hands on his hips. Finally, he stopped and looked at Danny.

"What do the deer do when they come upon something they don't understand?"

"They are frightened and run away." Danny answered.

"What do the grizzlies, the giant apes and men like Tarzan do, when they don't understand something?"

"Investigate?"

"Investigate, come to a reasonable conclusion, and put it behind them. Are you a frightened deer, or a man like Tarzan?"

"Tarzan wouldn't growl at a woman, watching him eat a piece of meat."

"Tarzan is a fictional character. In real life, he probably would have growled, too."

"I want to go back to the mountains."

The professor began pacing again, hands on hips, looking up at the ceiling, then down at the floor. This time, when he stopped to face Danny, he pointed a quivering finger at the boy's face. The professor's voice was shaking with emotion.

"Every day I stare into a sea of sleepy, yawning faces. Some are bored, others are polite, and some are downright blank. Once in a while, a timid hand goes up and a question is asked, giving me a ray of hope that perhaps something is happening in at least a few of those sleepy faces. Then one day, I witness a miracle."

"You told me, you don't believe in miracles," Danny objected.

"I don't believe in the claptrap, mumbo jumbo kind, that churches shove down people's throats. But the miracle of learning, the light of learning that only, once in a while, goes on in a young mind, is the miracle that keeps me going. The other morning, after thirty-five years of teaching at the college, I witnessed the greatest miracle of my career in a boy from the mountains, who stayed up all night, wrestling with a book, far too difficult for him to understand.

"You must believe me when I tell you that all the things you have learned and experienced in the mountains and in this library are but a few pine needles in an entire forest of ideas and experiences available to you if you will but continue down the path you have so nobly begun. You can't see it now, but you must have faith in what I am telling you."

"You told me, men of science and reason don't need faith," Danny responded.

"You read a few books and you think you can debate with a college professor. You know very well I was talking about the mumbo jumbo faith wasted on Santa Claus and fairy tales, the kind that tramples on science and reason. Now, I'm talking about faith of a different kind, faith in me as your mentor, faith in yourself and your potential."

"I don't think you can stop me," Danny challenged, "if I want to go back to the mountains."

"If you go back to the mountains, I will kill myself," the professor warned, shaking his big finger in Danny's face, once again. "But before I do, I will poison every bear in the forest. Now what do you have to say about that?"

Danny didn't know how to respond, so he

remained silent, his eyes wide, filled with the energy of the moment.

Once again, the professor was pacing back and forth, looking up and down, hands on hips. Danny couldn't imagine what was coming next.

"It is time to be like Tarzan, to confront the great apes of the forest," the professor said, as he turned to face Danny.

"I don't understand."

"It is time to learn to be like Tarzan, to face and confront the things that frighten and confuse you."

"I still don't understand."

"It is time to take the boy who grew up with the bears, and throw him to the lions."

"What does that mean?"

"Tomorrow, you will go to public high school."

Chapter 15

The next morning, as the professor was driving Danny to school, he tried to explain that human children are sometimes as inclined to hurt each other as are the animals of the forest, and that Danny should be very careful.

"They will try to hurt me?" Danny asked.

"I hope not," the professor responded, "but they can be very mean with words. They might tease you, try to make you feel bad."

"How will they do that?"

"Lots of ways. Maybe someone will say something that means something else. You don't understand, so they laugh at you, making you feel stupid."

"Why would anybody want to say something that means something else?"

"That's what people do. I haven't been in a public school for a long time, but among the adults I work with, when someone says we can't afford to get sentimental about something, it usually means they want to do something cruel. When someone says it's time to get practical, they are usually talking about making money."

"It seems stupid, saying one thing when you mean something else," Danny observed.

"Do you remember when we talked about the basic elements of the universe–hydrogen, oxygen, lead, iron– those kinds of things?" the professor asked.

"Yes."

"Did I ever tell you what the two most abundant elements in the universe are?"

"No."

"Hydrogen and stupidity. We can't do anything about the supply of hydrogen in the universe, but we have schools to help reduce stupidity. Sometimes, they don't do a very good job, so be careful."

Danny's throat was tight and his stomach was churning, as they walked up the front steps of the huge, brick building. Danny didn't think he had ever been inside such a large building before. Hundreds of young people, mostly his own age, were hurrying in every direction—boys and girls. They didn't seem to notice Danny, who was wearing store-bought slacks, shirt and shoes.

As they approached the principal's office, the professor offered one more caution.

"Most of the students here are Mormons. If you want to get along, you must respect their religious beliefs–even when they start talking about angels, gold plates, and leaders who don't make mistakes."

"How do I do that?"

"I respect a man's religious beliefs, the same way I respect his opinion that his wife is faithful and his children are smart. I just keep my mouth shut."

"I can do that."

"If you are asked about your religious beliefs, things will go better for you if you, don't tell them you lean towards atheism, at least not now. Wait until you are accepted, and a little better versed in what you believe. Do you understand?"

"You are telling me it's time to start learning to say one thing when you mean something different, like we talked about earlier."

Stopping in front of the principal's door, the professor handed Danny some lunch money. "I think you will do just fine," he said, winking at Danny before saying good-by and heading back to the college.

In the first class Danny had the opportunity to practice what he and the professor had talked about. The teacher asked him to go to the front of the room and tell a little bit about himself and the place where he had last lived.

As Danny walked slowly to the front of the class, he figured he was more frightened than the time the two cougars had chased him back to the den, and he didn't know why. While the cougars intended to eat him, no one here wanted to do that. There was no reason to feel so much fear. Still, the feeling would not go away.

"I lived with my brother, Ephraim, in the mountains," he began. Nobody laughed or made fun of him. So far, so good.

"We ate a lot of elk and deer meat, even fish, but my favorite food is lamb." Still no one laughed, though some of the boys began showing their lack of interest by doing other things.

"In the winter, we lived in a cave."

"I don't believe that for one minute," one of the boys in the back blurted out. "Why would anyone want to live in a cave?"

The teacher didn't interrupt. The class was silent, as everyone waited for Danny to respond.

"It is easier to stay warm in a cave, even without a fire," Danny offered. "You are safe from dangerous animals, like cougars."

"I still don't believe you," the same boy said.

"I believe him," someone else responded. It was a female voice, coming from a girl with golden curls, wearing a light blue dress. Looking at her, Danny felt the blood rising to his neck and face. She was the girl he had growled at in the market. In school she appeared even more beautiful, and she was on his side in the argument, even though he had growled at her in the store. At least, one person believed his story. Suddenly, feeling a boldness he had not felt before, Danny decided to move his presentation to a new level.

"How many of you have dogs and horses?" Danny asked. "Almost every hand in the class went up. "When I lived in the cave, I had a grizzly bear for a pet, a full-grown, sheep-killing grizzly. If you set your dogs on him, he would kill them all. Sometimes, I would ride him like you ride your horses."

Everyone in the class was talking and shouting, at the same time. The boy in the back was yelling, "Liar, liar, liar."

In their excitement, some of the students were

standing up. Danny was grinning, wondering what he could tell them next. He guessed, the pretty girl in the blue dress was really impressed with him now.

Finally, the teacher stood up, ordering everyone to stop talking and return to their desks, including Danny. The presentation was over.

"We are fortunate that our new student has a vivid imagination," the teacher said, when everyone was back in their seats, and the talking had ceased. "Those of you in the journalism club might invite Danny to join. Good writers need lots of imagination, and we all know, now, that Danny has plenty of that."

Danny spent the rest of the morning listening to lectures on various academic subjects. While he understood much of what was being taught, he found himself making frequent mental notes of things he wanted to ask the professor. He didn't dare raise his hand in class like some of the other students. In each new class, he was introduced as the school's newest student, but none of the other teachers invited him to go to the front of the class and tell about himself.

At noon, hundreds of students gathered in the lunchroom which was also the gym. Most of the students had brought food from home, usually in brown paper bags. The students who did not bring lunches were lining up at a window to buy hot dogs for a nickel each.

Danny was headed for the hot dog line, when he felt a tap on the shoulder. It was the golden-haired girl who had believed his story about the cave.

"I have an extra sandwich," she said, carefully. "One of my friends has some extra cookies. Would you like to join us?" She pointed to a table occupied by three girls.

"Your wish is my command," Danny said without thinking, immediately wondering how a phrase like that had come to mind.

"What did you say?" she asked softly, but with an intensity that made time stand still.

"Your wish is my...what is your name?" he asked, finally able to look into her deep, blue eyes without flinching.

"Ella. Ella Cowley. I live in Providence," she answered, her voice still soft, but electric. The thing he had said about her wish being his command, like a key, had opened up something new, something hidden inside her heart. Danny followed Ella to the table where they joined the three other girls, who were giggling and laughing.

Ella Cowley. Danny wondered where he had heard that name before.

"Did you live in the cave all the time, or was it just a temporary thing, like a place to stay on camping trips?" one of the girls asked before Danny could take a seat.

"We just camped there in the winter," Danny said, as he sat down.

"See, I told you," the girl said to the others.

"I'll bet the bear you talked about was a baby," the same girl said.

"The first time I saw him, he was just a cub," Danny responded, "no bigger than a dog. He wasn't dangerous at all. I didn't try to ride him until he got big."

"If you had said you raised him from a baby, some of the boys might have believed you," the girl added.

"What do we have to eat?" Danny asked, wanting to change the subject.

"Tuna on Wonder bread," Ella said, handing him a sandwich.

"What's Wonder bread?" Danny asked. The girls giggled at each other, finding it truly amazing that there was someone in the world who didn't know the meaning of Wonder bread. Danny didn't mind them laughing at him. Their intent seemed kind.

"Wonder bread is made in a factory," one of the girls explained. "Holds together better than home-made bread. Has lots of things in it that make you strong and healthy."

"Is that true?" Danny asked, looking at Ella.

"That's what they say on the radio," she responded.

"But you don't believe it?"

"I used to, but I had a dream. All my friends were getting skinny and pale from eating too much Wonder bread. In fact...."

"Whoa, hold your horses," one of the girls interrupted. Let's don't get Ella going on another dream."

"Why not?" Danny asked.

"Because she has weird dreams every night. Get her going and she can't stop. Right Ella?"

"Right," Ella said, looking down at the unfinished portion of her Wonder bread sandwich. "I'm sorry."

As Danny took a big bite from his sandwich, one of the girls pushed two big sugar cookies in his direction. Another handed him a carton of milk. Danny was enjoying this first contact with females his own age, so much, that he did not notice how some of the boys across the room were scowling at him.

When the bell sounded at the end of the school day, Danny felt drained. There was so much to think about. He had so many questions for the professor. He hurried down the front steps and across the school lawn, intending to run all the way home.

He had barely left the schoolyard, when he found himself surrounded by a group of boys his own age, maybe six or seven. He stopped, rather than try to push past them.

At first, none of the boys said anything. They stared at Danny, apparently sizing him up, and he stared back at them. Danny felt sick to his stomach, thinking that if he could get outside the circle he could probably outrun these boys. But he didn't know if they wanted to hurt him, or if the circle, was just some sort of get-acquainted ritual. He decided to wait and see. Finally, the biggest of the boys spoke.

"We don't like the lie you told about having a sheep-eating grizzly," he said. Danny did not respond.

"And we don't like you having lunch with Ella

Cowley," the boy continued. "She's my girl."

"I'd like to go home, now," Danny said, fighting to control a tremor in his voice.

"We'd like you to go home, too," the big boy said.

"Yeah, in a box," a smaller boy said. All of them laughed, except Danny.

"Before we let you go, you have to say two things," the bully continued. "Tell us you are sorry you lied about the grizzly bear. Then tell us you will never again have lunch with Ella Cowley. Say these two things and you can go."

Danny didn't know whether to fight or run. He knew only that he would not say the things he was being ordered to say.

When the big boy stepped forward into Danny's face, Danny stepped back. A mistake. Danny's attention had been so focused on the bully that he hadn't noticed how one of the other boys had dropped to his hands and knees directly behind Danny's legs. Danny found himself off balance, falling over backwards, while the boys laughed at him again.

Danny was on his feet in a second, crouching, his eyes narrowed to fiery orbs, his upper lip curled back, a rumbling sound emerging from deep in his chest as the big boy lunged forward to give him a beating.

Danny ducked to miss the first blow, then responded with a powerful sweep of his right hand, the same way Ephraim used his paw to break the neck or back of a running elk. The bully went down with Danny on top—hitting, twisting, tearing and even biting.

Soon, all was still, Danny on top, holding tightly to both of his opponent's ears, one of which was bleeding badly. When one of the other boys started forward to help the bully, Danny growled a warning. "One more step and I'll have your ears, too." The boy stepped back.

"Let go," the bully whined. "Please, let me go."

"Say 'Danny Evans has the meanest grizzly bear in Cache Valley,'" Danny hissed. When the boy didn't obey, Danny tightened his grip on the ears. More blood oozed from the injured ear.

"Danny Evans has the meanest bear in Cache Valley," the bully whined. "Now, please, let me go."

"I didn't hear you," Danny responded. The boy repeated what he had said in a louder voice, but still whining.

"Now, tell me that Danny Evans can have lunch with Ella Cowley whenever he wants to," Danny ordered. The boy quickly obeyed.

Danny let go of the ears and jumped to his feet. The other boys stepped back, giving Danny plenty of room. Before leaving, Danny spit a piece of bloody skin and some hair into his hand. He couldn't remember taking a bite out of the bully's ear during the fight, but apparently he had done just that.

"I prefer tuna on Wonder bread," Danny said, slinging the bloody remains onto the ground.

Suddenly feeling an urgent need to urinate, Danny stepped up to the nearest tree, unzipped his trousers, and began to go. It wasn't until he finished and turned around, that he realized about half the students in the school were watching and laughing. What could be funny about relieving oneself on a tree? Not understanding, he shrugged his shoulder and began to walk away.

That's when he noticed the Model T Ford stopping at the edge of the street. Ella Cowley was driving. Nobody else was in the car.

"Need a ride home?" she asked, after rolling down the window.

"Your wish is my command," he said. Both of them were laughing, as he ran around to the passenger side and climbed in.

"I remember where I heard that before," Ella said, before shifting into first gear. "I was little. There was a plate of cookies on the counter, too high for me to reach. I asked a neighbor boy to get one for me. He told me my wish was his command." She shifted into gear and headed up the road.

"Then you told the boy you were going to marry him," Danny added. "In the temple."

"It had something to do with a dream," she pondered. "That's all I remember. I was very sad when the boy was killed."

"The boy was Danny Evans. That's me. I was not killed—only my mother. I lived in the mountains, but now I am back."

"So what do we do now?" she asked, stopping the car in front of the professor's house.

"I don't know," Danny said, as he opened the door. "I've been gone a long time."

Chapter 16

That evening, Danny found himself alone in the study, curled up in the big chair with a Jack London novel. The professor had gone back to school to teach a night class. Rita had gone home after cleaning up the supper dishes.

Danny loved to escape into the pages of a novel, but on this particular evening, he found the scenes in London's story being replaced with scenes of Logan High School: the presentation in the first class, lunch with Ella and the girls, the struggle to understand and remember the things teachers were saying, the fight after school, and the ride home, when he and Ella remembered an earlier encounter, many years ago, when they were small children.

Suddenly, he was brought back to the present by a loud knocking on the front door. It was unusual to have guests in the evening. He hurried to the door, opening it wide. It was Ella, holding an old newspaper in her hand. She seemed excited. He invited her in.

"After dropping you off this afternoon, I went down to the newspaper office and looked through the archive," she explained. "I found this." She opened the newspaper. On the front, Danny saw the headline: "Woman's remains found in snowbank in Logan Canyon."

Ella began reading from the article. "'Authorities found the partially decomposed body of Arlene Evans in a snowbank at the top of Logan Canyon. Mrs. Evans had been dead for some time....Authorities said the woman had disappeared from her Logan home in November....Authorities believe her six-year-old son, Danny, was with her at the time of the accident. The search continues for the boy's remains, but police suspect the boy was carried off by wild animals.... Funeral services for mother and son will be held....'"

"You're dead!" Ella said, looking up at Danny.

Danny had first seen Ella in the market, then in class that morning, again at lunch, and after school, but never had she looked so beautiful as at this very moment. As she began to read something else from the newspaper, Danny bent forward and kissed her on the cheek. She didn't pull away, but turned until her lips met his. They both stood very still for a moment that seemed forever, but was not long enough.

"The article was wrong," she whispered, finally breaking the silence. "You are not dead, but very much alive...."

Suddenly, the front door opened. The professor had come home.

"This is Ella Cowley," Danny stammered, stepping away from her, both their faces very red. "She found an old newspaper article, telling how my mother and me were killed."

"Nice to meet you, Ella," the professor said in a cheery voice. "I'd love to see that article. Let's go in the kitchen. I brought home some ice cream."

Life fell into a routine for Danny. He began taking notes in class so he could remember what the teachers had said. In the evenings, in addition to his regular reading, he read the school assignments, did the math, and studied for exams. He spent the noon hour with Ella. They shared lunches—except when he surprised her with a raw lamb chop. Sometimes, her friends joined them, but most of the time they were alone.

Some of the boys began to befriend Danny. After the fight, the bullies left him alone. The coach, Mr. Romney, invited Danny to stay after school and practice with the football team, which was undefeated. At first, Danny declined, fearing that if he became engaged in aggressive contact with other players, he might forget himself, as he had done in the fight with the bully, and bite off part of another ear.

But when Danny learned that leather helmets covered the ears of the players, he decided to give it a try. Since Danny had no skill in handling the ball, the coach assigned him to the linebacker position on defense. The instructions were simple: "Don't move until the ball is hiked, then catch and bring down the man with the ball."

Danny began practicing with the team every day. The rough and tumble activity felt good, reminding him of the early years in the mountains when Ephraim was still young and playful.

But Danny soon learned that the game of football was more complicated than he at first thought. The first time the coach let him in a real game, one of his teammates intercepted a pass. At first, Danny couldn't figure out why everyone was yelling at him, when he caught the man with the ball and brought him down. After that, the coach would not let Danny play until the outcome of the game had already been decided.

Sometimes after practice, he would hang out with some of his new friends. Sometimes, they would go to the Cherry Blossom for candy, then drive up and down Main Street in a Model T belonging to one of the boys' fathers. Other times, they would drive up one of the nearby canyons to sip moonshine from a stone jug or practice smoking. Danny was willing to try anything. He didn't tell Ella or the professor what he was doing.

Between school, football practice, hanging out with his new friends, and trying to finish homework assignments, Danny found he no longer had time to read. He didn't feel bad because none of his friends had time for reading beyond their school assignments, either.

In school, Danny's favorite class was English. The teacher, Mrs. Morrell, loved Danny's short essays. He wrote descriptions of things that had happened to him in the mountains, like being chased by the two cougars, the first time he nursed the mother bear, he and Ephraim killing sheep by the light of a full moon.

At first, Mrs. Morrell praised Danny for his vivid imagination, but in time, she realized the source of his material was not imagination. There was too much detail. The stories were too believable. She insisted Danny join the journalism club and start writing for the school newspaper, *The Avesta*.

Danny's first published article was about the hibernating habits of grizzly bears. A controversy was stirred up when the school received a letter from a biology professor at the college, objecting to Danny's claim that hibernating bears did not defecate or urinate during hibernation. The professor said this was not true, and the *Avesta* editor, Ernest Oldham, insisted on publishing the letter that was calling Danny a liar.

Oldham also insisted that Danny write a rebuttal to accompany the professor's attack. Danny's response was short, saying only that it was obvious that the grizzly expert at the Utah Agricultural College had never visited the den of a hibernating grizzly, but if he wished to do so, Danny knew the location of a den, they could visit together. Nothing more was heard from the professor, and it seemed the students in the school were all on Danny's side. Life seemed to be getting better every day.

A few days after the hibernating controversy had settled down, Ella asked Danny to go to the homecoming dance with her. He wasn't sure what he was saying yes to. She told him that following the afternoon football game, three of her friends, with their dates, would go to Ella's home in Providence for dinner. After eating, they would return to the school to the dance.

"But I don't know how to dance," Danny objected.

"You won't be alone," she answered. "Most of the boys don't know how to dance, either, but by the time the evening is over, you will know how to do it. I will teach you."

"What's for dinner?" Danny asked.

"Your favorite, leg of lamb."

"Then, I'll go," he responded, cheerfully.

Danny was feeling proud and handsome when two of the boys picked him up for the drive over to Providence on homecoming day. For the first time in his life, Danny was wearing a dress suit with a white shirt and tie, and new black shoes, which the professor had polished until they shown like the paint on the hood of a new car.

As soon as the car started down the street, one of the boys screwed the cap off a bottle of beer, which the boys began to pass around. Losing track of time, the boys arrived late in Providence.

The girls were already seated at the table. A steaming leg of lamb was resting on a white platter in the middle of the table. It looked and smelled good, though Danny would have preferred it without the cooking. There were mashed potatoes, gravy, carrots, fresh-baked rolls, linen napkins, dishes of pickles and olives, and some red wiggly stuff which he later learned was gelatin.

Before taking their seats at the table, Ella introduced Danny to her father, a stern-looking gentleman with very little hair and a sagging paunch, then to her mother. Both parents were dressed like they were going to church. They seemed more careful than warm, as they greeted him and shook his hand. Danny had the feeling, Ella had not told them very much about him.

Ella had never looked more beautiful. She was wearing a pink, satin, sheath-type dress that fit her perfectly, and a matching headband. Her golden hair seemed more curled than usual. Danny thought, she looked better than a picture in a magazine.

When Danny and Ella were seated with the other couples, Ella's sisters, wearing white aprons, brought in salads on little plates—one for each person.

Danny was prepared. The professor had coached him, carefully, on how to use his fork, spoon and knife, instead of his hands; where to place the napkin; to be generous with "please" and "thank you;" not to chew with his mouth open, or pick his teeth or his nose. He felt ready, filled with a warm glow, thanks to the beer, he and his friends had been drinking.

But, Danny was not prepared for what happened next. Ella's father stepped into the doorway and asked Danny to say a blessing on the food. The warm glow disappeared. Danny didn't know what to say. His mind was empty.

He wanted to impress Ella's parents, but didn't know how they blessed their food. He couldn't remember how his parents had done it when he was little, only how Professor Nibley did it. Had Danny not been drinking the beer, it might have occurred to him that the professor's style of praying might raise a few eyebrows in a regular Mormon household.

Danny looked around, hoping someone might offer a little help. All eyes were closed, all heads bowed, even those belonging to family members not seated at the table. Danny was too scared to think. The only phrases in his mind were the ones he remembered the professor using to mock organized religion.

"Dear God," Danny said, after closing his eyes and bowing his head. "Who so loved the world that he cursed most of his children with disease, pestilence and war....Please send us a raw leg of lamb to go with this cooked one, so we will know you really do exist and answer prayers." Danny could hear a couple of the boys pushing air through their nasal passages, but it was too late to stop now. "We thank you for this food, even though Mrs. Cowley bought it at the store. Amen."

Hearing the uneasy whispering around him, Danny didn't want to open his eyes. When he did, Ella's father was glaring at him from across the table. The sisters and mother had disappeared.

"Blasphemy," was all the father said, before ordering Ella to say a proper blessing, which she promptly did. Her father was not seen during the remainder of the dinner. Ella seemed sad. The conversation of the other couples seemed forced. The food tasted bland and cold. Danny figured he had made a terrible mistake, and didn't know how to fix it.

In an effort to cheer things up, he asked what the fish said when it swam into the cement wall. The looks on the other faces were blank, even when Danny said "dam."

When they got up from the table to return to the dance, Danny found himself face to face with Ella's father.

"How dare you come into this home and offend our Lord and Savior," the father complained. "I don't want you seeing my daughter, any more. Is that clear?"

"If I offended your Lord and Savior, maybe He should be the one to tell me so, not you," Danny said, looking down at his feet. He turned and followed the other couples to the waiting cars. Danny had no intention of staying away from Ella. That, he would not do—not unless Ella wished him to do so.

As soon as they arrived at the dance, Ella suggested they go by themselves to one of the tables against the far wall, where they could talk in private.

"Are you an atheist?" she asked, even before they had taken their seats.

"I have read a book that is forbidden in our school library: Darwin's *Origin of the Species*. I have read it twice, and I agree with Darwin's conclusions."

"You are avoiding my question? Do you believe in God?"

"I spent ten years in the mountains, a place you people call God's country. I have good eyes, but I never saw him. I have good ears, but I never heard his voice. You want me to believe in a God I never met. I don't know how to do that."

"So, you admit to being an atheist?"

"No, but perhaps an agnostic. If God speaks to me and tells me to believe in Him, I will do it. I do not say He does not exist, only that He has never made His reality known to me."

"You know nothing of faith," she said, a pleading tone in her voice. Danny thought her eyes were more moist than normal.

"I have faith, the sun will come up in the morning," he said, "And that, in the winter, the mountains will be full of snow."

"I am amazed that a young man with no brains can sound so smart," she said.

"I have brains just like everyone else."

"Have you ever seen them?"

"No."

"Have you ever touched them, or smelled them, or heard them?"

"What are you trying to say?" he asked.

"I am trying to reason like you do. The same logic that leads you to believe there is no God, leads me to believe you have no brains."

"Would you like to dance?" he asked, hoping to change the subject.

"No," she said, tears freely running down her cheeks. "I thought it was a miracle when you said my wish was your command. It was like fate, or destiny, or God bringing us together in some kind of wonderful miracle."

"I felt the same way."

"Ever since I was a little girl," she continued, fighting for control of her emotions, "I've known that, someday, I would be married in the house of the Lord, that temple on the hill. A young man who believes in God and miracles will take me there. You are not that man, Danny Evans."

"They would probably let me in if I lied," he said, more harshness in his voice than he intended. She started to get up.

"Where are you going?" he asked.

"To the telephone, to call my father to come and get me."

"Please stay," he begged.

"Good-by, Danny Evans. Have a nice life," were her last words, as she disappeared into the crowd.

Danny spent the remainder of the evening with his other friends. Occasionally, the boys would slip out to the cars where they had stashed some moonshine and beer. When it was finally time to go home, Danny's friends had to carry him up the steps and lean him against the professor's door.

Sometime in the night, Danny awakened, staring through the frosty window above his bed, hoping sleep would return to numb the throbbing pain in his head and chest.

Chapter 17

Over the weekend, Danny stayed pretty much to himself, thinking and catching up on homework assignments. He wanted to return to the mountains, but with winter on its way, he knew life would be more interesting in high school—even without the company of Ella Cowley—than in a den with a snoring bear.

He kept wondering what he might have done differently to preserve the relationship with Ella. If only he had been alert enough to decline the request to bless the food, but it was too late to change any of that, now.

When Danny arrived at school Monday morning, everyone was talking about an eight-year-old girl, Molly Burgess, who had been lost in the mountains over the weekend. She had been with her family in a hunting camp up the right hand fork of the Logan River. She had gone for a horseback ride by herself. The horse had returned to camp, but not the girl.

With the cold nights and approaching winter storms, everyone in the community was concerned. A storm had already wiped out the horse's tracks.

Search parties had gone out, and more were being organized, including one at the school.

Danny was one of the first to sign up. He grew up in the country where the missing girl had last been seen. He knew many good places to look for her. It would feel good to be in the mountains again. Maybe, he could help rescue the girl.

Danny was told to go home and change into winter clothing, including snow boots and a warm coat and hat, and to fill his pockets with food. If possible, he was instructed to bring a rifle and binoculars. He was told there were grizzly bears in the area and that as many searchers as possible should be armed. He was told to report back at the school at 1:00 p.m. A truck would carry the search party to the mountains.

The professor came home at noon and helped Danny find some snow boots that fit. After filling Danny's pockets with sandwiches, cookies, boiled eggs, and apples, the professor drove him back to the school.

As they came to a stop in front of the building, the other searchers were standing in a circle, hats off, heads bowed, while one of the teachers offered a prayer. The professor turned off the motor.

"Do you think prayers do any good?" Danny asked.

"Of course," the professor responded. "When people are embarking on something like this, where the chances of success are very slim, at best, people are more likely to work harder if they think God is helping or guiding them."

"Do you think they are doing the right thing, sending out all these boys to look for the girl?"

"Of course. The life of a child is priceless."

"Nobody searched for me when I was lost in the mountains."

"Nobody knew you were lost. Your father thought your mother had taken you to Wyoming. It wasn't until the following spring that they learned the car had rolled off the road. After that much time, everyone assumed you were dead."

Several hours later, Danny and about thirty other boys from the school, were spread out in a long line, moving horizontally along a steep hillside, a boy every twenty feet or so. There was a teacher at each end of the line, and one in the middle. They pushed their way across several hillsides before the sun went down and it was too dark to continue.

When the boys returned to the trucks, they found a huge tent and a milk can full of chili, simmering over an open fire. After eating, the boys were given sleeping bags which they rolled out side by side in the tent. Danny kept thinking how much fun all this would be if there wasn't a lost girl to worry about.

The next day, the group worked further and further from camp, pushing through thick stands of timber, marshes, and along rocky, brush-covered hillsides. It made Danny nervous that so many of the boys carried guns. He hoped Ephraim didn't get in their path. They found no sign of the girl, not even a track. No horse tracks either, except for some old sign where a sheepherder had camped.

Some of the searchers were beginning to believe the girl had met with foul play.

By the end of the day, the boys were tired, and many wanted to go home. The weary search party was trucked back to Logan.

The next morning, Danny was more than a little surprised when Ella stepped in front of him as he entered the school. This was the first time she had spoken to him since the dance. The silence was awkward as he waited for her to speak.

"Tell me about the search," she said.

"We covered a lot of country," Danny explained, "spread out in a long line, looking under every rock and bush, and behind every tree. No sign of the girl."

"Do you think she is still out there? Do you think she is still alive?"

"I don't know. If she was there, the search parties should have found her by now. If she's alive, someone should've heard her cries."

"Last night in my dreams, I saw a girl in a black and white coat who was nursing an injured leg. She was in a dark place..." Ella paused.

"And?"

"I thought it was just a dream. Then, this morning, someone told me the lost girl was wearing a black and white coat. I didn't know that before, but I had seen the black and white coat in my dream."

"Why are you telling me this?" Danny asked. "I am the last person who might believe in a vision or dream."

"I know. But near the dark place, where I saw

the girl, I saw a cross."

"Like on a church?"

"Yes."

"So, why tell all this to the most non-religious person you know?"

"You spent ten years in the mountains, the same place where the girl is lost. I thought maybe you had seen the cross, or something that looks like a cross."

"I already told you. I didn't find God, or a burning bush, or a cross, or anything else that seemed religious, except maybe a few sunsets." Danny started to leave. He was feeling angry, and hurt.

"In my dream, I saw a black and white coat. There has to be a reason."

"When you figure it out, let me know," he said, as he walked away.

In his first class, Danny could not listen to the teacher. He could think only of Ella and her stupid dream. She had looked so great. He had had that same feeling again, like at the market the first time he saw her, the warm blanket in a snowstorm. It had felt good to be close to her, to look at her, to smell her. He wished he had been bold enough to touch her hand.

Absentmindedly, he sketched a cross on the notepad in front of him. Why had she seen a cross? Catholic priests didn't come to these mountains to plant crosses. But, people put crosses on graves. Maybe the lost girl was by a grave. In all his wanderings during those ten years in the mountains, Danny had seen some graves, mostly Indian graves, mounds of rocks, but none of them had crosses on top....

Then he remembered the two dead trees that formed the big *t*. He had never thought of the *t* as a cross, but a cross and a *t* were the same. Without asking permission, he got up and walked out of class.

Two doors down the hall, Ella was in math class. Danny peeked through the partially opened door, caught her attention, then motioned for her to come out in the hall. In three or four seconds, she was standing in front of him.

"I know a place where two trees make a big *t*. Never thought of it as a cross before."

She closed her eyes, as if trying to remember something. "I think the parts of the cross were rounded, like trees," she said, finally opening her eyes.

"Nearby, there's a cave," he explained, "maybe the dark place you saw."

"Do you think I'm crazy?" she asked.

"I don't know how to explain the black and white coat."

"How long would it take to get there?" she asked.

"Do you have the car?"

"Yes."

"It's nine, now, and it won't be dark until six. We could be there by five, if we hurried."

"Don't turn here," Danny said, when she began to turn off the main road into Right Hand Fork.

"But, this is the way to the hunting camp, where the girl was last seen. My father said the search parties went this way."

"I know, but the cave with the big cross is closer to the end of the Temple Fork road."

An hour later, they were hiking up one of the trails used almost entirely by wild animals, but Danny knew it well. The snowfall had been much lighter than usual for this time of year, so they made good time. Ella wasn't as strong as Danny, so occasionally, he had to wait for her to catch up, but he wasn't about to leave her behind.

The sun was just setting beyond the western foothills, when Danny pointed out the two trees that formed the big cross. Then he pointed to the den entrance. There was no sign of the girl.

"Better stay back," Danny warned, as they approached the cave. "Might be a bear inside." Ella obeyed.

"Anybody home?" Danny called into the cave, his voice quiet and pleasant.

There was no response, not even the growl of a bear. Danny crawled inside. In the waning light, it was difficult to see, but Danny's eyes adjusted quickly. Ephraim was sleeping in the usual place, his back against the rear wall. The girl in the black and white coat was sleeping, too, snuggled against Ephraim's soft, warm belly.

Danny crawled out of the cave to get Ella. "You've got to see this," he said, taking her by the hand, and pulling her behind him into the dark hole. Danny pulled a flashlight out of his pocket and turned it on. Ella placed both hands over her mouth in a look of complete astonishment.

After handing the flashlight to Ella, Danny knelt beside the girl. "Molly," he said, "Wake up. We have come to take you home."

When Molly finally opened her eyes and found herself face to face with a total stranger, she quickly pulled away, snuggling closer to the furry bear who continued to sleep. "Who are you?" she asked in a timid voice.

"I'm Danny, and this is Ella. We came to take you home," he said, in a smooth and reassuring voice.

"But, I can't walk," she said. "My leg hurts awful bad."

For the first time, Danny noticed how Molly's riding pants were stretched tight over a swollen knee.

"Would you like something to eat before we put a splint on your leg?" Ella asked.

"I'm not hungry," Molly said.

"But you've been here three days," Ella said.

"I found cans of sardines and a jar of apple-sauce," Molly explained, pointing to the other side of the cave, "and a canteen full of water."

While Danny and Ella were fashioning a splint from two sticks and an old sheepherder shirt, Molly told them her story.

She was riding her horse through the valley below the cave, when she caught sight of something brown and furry moving into the entrance of the cave. If she had known it was a bear, she would not have ridden her horse up the hill to investigate.

She wasn't very far from the cave entrance, when the big bear stuck his head out to see who was coming. The horse panicked, rearing over backwards, crushing Molly's knee in the fall, and then galloped back to camp without her.

Molly said she was screaming in terror when the big bear came out of the cave and walked down to her. She was sure the beast was going to eat her. At least kill her. Instead, it licked her face. Then it laid down beside her, continuing to lick her face, then her hands, then its own paws.

Sometime that first night, the bear grabbed the edge of her coat in his mouth and dragged her to the cave. Once inside, the bear stretched out against the back wall and went to sleep. By now, Molly realized the bear did not want to hurt her. She curled up against the warm fur and went to sleep, too. When the morning sun made the cave, light enough to see, Molly found the water and food. The bear continued to sleep as he was sleeping, now.

By the time the splint was finished, it was dark outside. There was no moon, and storm clouds were blocking the light from the stars.

"I think we should wait until morning," Danny said.

"And if the bear wakes up?" Ella asked.

"He has already demonstrated that he has no desire to eat Molly," Danny warned, a sparkle in his eye, "and I know he has no desire to eat me. But Ella Cowley, who knows?"

"I'm going home," Ella said, crawling towards

the cave opening. "I don't care if it's dark outside."

Danny rolled forward, grabbing her foot, pulling her back.

"I was just teasing," he said.

"Not funny. I'm still going home."

"I've spent ten years with hibernating bears," Danny explained. "From the way he's breathing, and with this thick layer of fat, there's no reason for him to wake up any time soon, especially not tonight."

"You're sure?"

"Absolutely."

Cautiously, she moved back to her place beside Danny and Molly. Danny turned off the light, explaining he wanted to save the batteries in case they needed them in the middle of the night.

With their backs against Ephraim's warm belly, Danny began telling stories about the adventures he and Ephraim had had over the years. Molly was the first to fall asleep. Ella slept little, if any. Danny dozed off from time to time, but awoke frequently to make sure the girls were all right. He tried to imagine what it would be like, living in the mountains with a woman and a child to take care of, to keep him company. A pretty good life, he thought—perhaps paradise.

Fortunately, there was just a dusting of new snow during the night. At first light, they headed down the trail, Ella leading the way, Danny following close behind, Molly riding piggyback.

Traveling downhill, they made good time. When they had covered about half the distance, they came upon a group of armed men following their tracks from the day before. As the men got closer, they could see Ella's father in the lead, a shotgun in his right hand, his face red with anger.

The angry father shouldered past his surprised daughter without even saying Goodmorning, and was in Danny's face, shouting, "I told you to stay away...."

By this time, the other men had spotted the little face looking over Danny's shoulder, and were joyously pushing past Ella and her father to get a better look. The little girl that was lost—the little girl everyone was looking for—the little girl everyone feared was dead—was not dead, but very much alive.

"It was dark when we found her," Ella explained. "We had to spend the night in a cave." Danny was glad she did not mention Ephraim. These men would probably want to go to the cave and shoot the bear that had frightened Molly's horse.

With so many people around, Ella and Danny didn't have a chance to talk in private the rest of the day, but the next morning, she cornered him in the hall at school before class.

"I have just one question for you, Danny Evans," she said. There was warmth in her voice. The iciness of the prom night had not returned.

"I'm afraid to ask what it might be," he said, totally enjoying her warmth.

"How would you and your atheist friends explain the black and white coat I saw in my dream?"

"I don't have any atheist friends," he responded.

"Don't avoid my question," she warned. "Just

look me in the eye and tell me you don't believe some kind of divine power worked through me to save a little girl's life."

"I don't know what to say," he said, looking away.

"Your atheism looks like pretty shallow stuff in the light of yesterday's events," she said. "And I want to know what you are going to do about it?"

"I don't know," he said, looking back at her. "I just don't know."

"Well, I have some suggestions when you are ready to talk about it," she said, as the bell rang for classes to begin.

Chapter 18

"If she hadn't seen the black and white coat in her dream, and later learned that that is exactly what Molly was wearing, Ella might not have taken her dream seriously," Danny explained to the professor that evening. "If Ella hadn't seen the two trees forming the cross, I would not have known where to look for the girl. Seeing both things in a dream, can't be the result of chance."

The professor lit his pipe and placed his feet on the table before responding. "For years, people said if God intended for man to fly He would have given him wings. Then, the Wright brothers did it. The other day, I heard a woman claim that every time an airplane leaves the ground, two invisible angels come down from heaven, each grabbing a wing to make sure the plane doesn't crash. The woman can't understand the scientific basis of mechanical flight, so she gives the credit to God. That's a lot easier than learning aerodynamics."

"Do you think there's a scientific explanation for Ella's dream?"

The professor slowly placed his pipe in an ashtray, got up and walked over to the radio, an

Edison model with a rounded top. He turned it on, waited for a minute for it to warm up, then turned the tuning knob until he found a clear signal. The room filled with sound of singing, a weekly broadcast of the Mormon Tabernacle Choir in Salt Lake City.

"The choir is singing a hundred miles away, on the other side of some very large mountains," the professor explained. "As I understand it, when the people sing, waves in the air make a crystal vibrate. The vibration goes through an amplifier into the sky. That same radio signal starts a crystal vibrating in this little radio, and suddenly, the room is filled with music. That's how a radio works, but I'm sure we could find an old woman who would tell us that God wants the good people of Cache Valley to hear the choir, so his angels carry the signal over the mountains."

"What does all this have to do with Ella's dream?"

The professor returned to his chair and picked up his pipe.

"We have a little girl who falls off her horse and is dragged into a den by a bear. She thinks she is going to be his midnight snack. The emotional trauma generates enough energy to transmit some kind of bio-signal into the atmosphere. A short distance away in her bedroom in Providence, Ella is in a deep sleep. Ella, perfect in every way, is totally relaxed, receptive to the tiniest vibrations in the atmosphere. There is no interference to block the tiny bio-signal from triggering a dream. Ella picks up some of the same information that has been going through the brain of the little girl up in the mountains."

"Do you believe that is what happened?" Danny asked.

"I honestly don't know. Stranger things have happened. But just because I can't explain Ella's dream, I don't make the quantum jump to divine miracles and run down to the tabernacle to get baptized so I can start paying tithing."

They both laughed. Danny hoped that someday he would be as smart as the professor.

"Ella wanted to know what I was going to do about the dream," Danny said. "I guess I'll tell her I'm going to join the Radio Club and study medicine, so I can better understand radio and brain waves."

"Be careful," the professor cautioned. "Don't forget the damage you did with that blessing on the food. You lost her. Now you have a small chance to get her back. Don't make another big mistake."

"I don't understand. You want me to be honest, don't you?"

"Yes, but careful, too."

"I don't understand."

"Do you think Charles Darwin was a great man?"

"You are changing the subject."

The professor repeated the question.

"I like his book."

"Darwin and Twain are my favorite authors. But roll them up in one package with a hundred more atheists, and the combined total isn't equal to the little toe of Ella Cowley, as far as Danny Evans is concerned."

"What are you saying?"

"That night she had ice cream with us, I saw the way she looked at you, and the way you looked at her. Some people go through an entire lifetime without finding that."

"Finding what?"

"The greatest happiness in the world is finding someone like Ella and being totally and completely in love. You love her. She loves you. And the rest of the world stands still."

"How would an old atheist like you know anything about that?" Danny asked, grinning. He knew the professor wasn't always serious, and this was probably one of those times, so he decided to throw a little sand in an old man's eye. "I doubt an old bachelor could begin to understand the love strings in the hearts of a couple of teen-agers."

Instead of offering a rebuttal, the professor got to his feet again and walked over to the bookshelf. He removed a photo album, one Danny had not noticed before. The professor opened it, showing Danny a photograph of a beautiful black-haired, young woman in a white dress. She was standing in front of the Logan Temple.

"Who is she?" Danny asked.

"Emma. My wife. You see, I wasn't always the salty, old bachelor you see before you."

"I didn't know you had a wife."

"Yes, and the few years we spent together were as close to paradise as two human beings in this life can get—at least that's the way I remember it. This might surprise you, but I was a God-fearing man at the time."

"What happened?"

"A growth in her brain. The doctor said he had to take the top of her skull off to remove the pressure. She never recovered. We anointed her with oil, and I said a hundred prayers. She died, anyway. The doctor went fishing, and I went to hell." Slowly, the professor closed the album, placed it back on the bookshelf, then returned to his chair.

"So, what do I do?" Danny asked. "Forget everything I've learned, pretend God spoke to me from heaven, then join her church?"

"No. If you lived a lie ,you wouldn't be worthy of her."

"So, what do I do?"

"Open your mind and heart. Listen to her. Read her scriptures. Go to church. Pray. If you have an open mind for her beliefs, perhaps she will have an open mind for yours. Give her a copy of Darwin's book."

"If I do this, what will happen?"

"I don't know. Maybe, you will accept, her way of believing. Maybe, she will accept yours. Maybe, you will find a middle ground where you can be happy together. That happens sometimes, you know."

Danny didn't sleep much that night. He thought a lot about what the professor had said—especially the revelation that the professor had once had a wife, and been a God-fearing man. Danny realized that the things people said, did not always give an accurate picture of what that person was really like inside. Danny hadn't known the professor was carrying a terrible sadness in his heart. The old man had covered it well, but, now, Danny found himself crying for the man who had become a father to him, the kind of father he had always hoped for, but never had.

The next day in the hall at school, Danny showed Ella the Bible he was reading in his free time. He told her that when he finished that, he intended to read the Book of Mormon, too. He told her that finding Molly, had opened his heart to a new searching that he hoped to follow to a rightful conclusion.

At the same time, he handed her his copy of *Origin of the Species* by Charles Darwin.

"Don't throw this in the trash," he cautioned. "I want you to read it, so you will understand some of the ideas that pull me in a different direction."

She slipped the book inside a brown binder, quickly looking over her shoulder to make sure no one was watching. "I will have to be careful that my father doesn't see it," she said.

"Speaking of your father," Danny said, "do you think he would allow you to have me over for dinner anytime soon?"

"He doesn't like you. He doesn't approve of me seeing you. Rescuing Molly didn't change anything."

"I just thought that if I came over, and said a proper blessing on the food, he might soften a bit."

Ella grinned. "You have a lot more courage

than I thought you had. I'll see what I can do."

Later that day, several of Danny's classmates encouraged him to try out for a part in the school's upcoming opera production, *Captain Crossbones*. Tryouts were to take place that same evening in the school gym. Danny declined. Practicing with the football team and writing for the school paper were about all he had time for. Besides, he really liked being part of the journalism club, and was starting to think that someday he would be a writer. Ernest Oldham had given him an assignment to attend a grazing association meeting on predator control, that same evening. He didn't want to miss that, especially when he heard that bear-killer, Frank Clark, was one of the speakers.

The meeting was held in the Tabernacle because there was plenty of room for all the farmers and ranchers who wanted to attend. Increased depredations on the part of cougars, wolves, coyotes and bears had stirred up a lot of concern on the part of livestock growers.

Several hundred people were in attendance—mostly men. As Danny looked around the audience, he recognized two faces: Tony Hunsaker, the young herder who had befriended him a few summers back, and Frank Clark, the bear-killer the deputies had stopped to talk to after arresting Danny. Because Clark was on the program, he was sitting up front, facing the audience. Danny took a seat by Tony, who broke the ice, by asking Danny if he knew what the fish said when he ran into the cement wall.

The first speaker was a biologist from the

college, who talked about new poisons that were proving very effective in other western states in controlling predators. He said the problem with poisons was that many non-targeted animals were killed: foxes, badgers, eagles, magpies, dogs, etc.

The next speaker was Frank Clark, who said he had killed eight bears the previous summer, and hoped to get another half dozen or so during the coming grazing season. He said, nearly 200 sheep were killed the past summer, but he guessed that number would be greatly diminished when a few more bears were caught. He claimed, a single grizzly was responsible for most of the dead sheep.

Clark's trapping methods included claw traps with bait. He didn't think poison, with all the associated risks, would be necessary. Some of the men in the audience applauded, while others grumbled.

Clark said the grizzly in question—easily identified by missing toes on a front foot—would sometimes kill eight or ten sheep in a night—many more than he could possibly eat. He guessed from the missing toes that the bear had been caught in a claw trap, before, somehow escaping. That would explain why the bear had so much skill in avoiding traps. Clark said, he had a nickname for this clever bear. He called him Old Ephraim, after a famous grizzly that harassed settlers for many years in a California settlement.

"Once, this old feller is gone, we won't be holding meetings like this," Clark said. "My main goal, this coming season, is to put a bullet in Old Ephraim's head. I won't rest until it's done. By this time next year, Old Ephraim will be history." The audience applauded, loudly. Danny felt sick to his stomach.

The next day, Danny wrote his article for the newspaper, but it was more of an editorial than a news article. He pointed out that predators, particularly grizzly bears, were forced to kill and eat sheep and cattle because white men had reduced the number of deer and elk. After all, the bears were in the mountains first, and if the white men were going to invade bear country, killing off the wild game, and then fill the mountains with thousands of sheep and cattle, they ought to be willing to pay for the grazing by donating a few sheep and cattle.

Danny pointed out that it was a good thing Frank Clark hadn't killed Old Ephraim the previous summer. Had that been the case, then Old Ephraim would not have been on hand to save little Molly by dragging her into his den and keeping her warm and safe until rescuers could come and get her. Danny said, he couldn't understand the bloodlust and greed that made men want to kill the gentle beast who had saved the life of a little girl.

Danny said, the only harm done to little Molly was the redness on her face where the bear had licked away her tears with his sandpaper tongue. It was the horse that had hurt her leg.

Danny was surprised at the reaction of his classmates. He was almost a hero, overnight. Students in the art classes were drawing pictures of grizzly bears. Students in English classes were writing essays demanding preservation of the grizzly. There was talk of changing the name of the newspaper to *The Grizzly*, and adopting Ephraim as the school mascot.

Danny wasn't surprised when some of the sheep growers wrote letters to the editor, strongly disagreeing with his defense of Old Ephraim. Editor Oldham insisted on printing every one of them. Publishing the attacks on Danny, only strengthened student support for grizzly bears.

Chapter 19

Winter turned into spring, and spring into summer. While school was still in session, Danny and Ella were together every day. Sometimes, in the evenings, he would go to her house to study, but more often, she would come to his. While the Cowley home was full of children and the accompanying confusion, the professor's home was quiet and more conducive to study, plus the professor liked Ella.

In fact, Danny sometimes wondered if the professor hadn't fallen in love with Ella, too. He always made sure there were good things to eat when she was around, and sometimes, he gave her presents–maybe a book or a bouquet of flowers. He gave her a new pair of earrings, and a bracelet, too. Danny and Ella would do homework, work on his articles, discuss things they were reading, or just sit on the front porch and listen to the radio. Sometimes, they would discuss the things Danny was reading in the Bible. One evening, he described to her how Elijah, in the First Book of Kings, had challenged the four hundred priests of Baal to a test that would prove who was the true God of Israel.

After the priests of Baal were unsuccessful in

getting their god to manifest himself by burning their sacrifice, Elijah then called down fire from heaven, which consumed his sacrifice after he had soaked it with water. All the people saw and believed, then killed the four hundred priests of Baal.

"If your church is true, your prophet should be able to do stuff like that," Danny said.

"If you saw fire come down from heaven, then you would believe?" she asked.

"Of course."

"That isn't going to happen, Danny, so I guess you'll always be an agnostic."

After this exchange, whenever the subject of religion came up, Danny tried to avoid another argument. His reading of the Bible, stopped at the end of the Elijah story. And he spent less and less time with Ella, and more time with the boys, driving up and down Main Street, drinking beer.

The professor frequently gave Ella things to read, the same as he did Danny, but the old man was never contentious when they discussed religion or philosophy. He never made fun of her religious beliefs.

But, the evenings together, ended the day school was out. Danny couldn't wait to get back to the mountains. He missed Ephraim, the fishing and hunting expeditions, the rigorous exercise, the wild diet, even the loneliness.

The professor helped Danny fill a pack with food, camping supplies, and books. He warned Danny against raiding the sheep and hunting camps, then drove Danny to the end of the road in Temple Fork.

"When will I see you again?" the professor asked, as Danny removed his things from the car.

"When I get hungry, or when school starts," Danny responded, cheerily.

"So, I can count on you to be with me for another school year?"

"That's my plan. I want to graduate, then go to college and study writing and journalism. I've decided to become a writer."

"You seem pretty sure of yourself."

"That's what I'm going to do. Maybe, I'll go to an eastern university."

"You don't seem nearly as excited about your spiritual quest. Lately, you and Ella don't talk much about the things you have been reading in the Bible. You've learned to say a proper blessing on the food, but I don't see anymore serious effort to get answers."

"Wait a minute," Danny said, a hint of anger in his voice. "Cache Valley's spokesman for atheism is getting after me for not being interested in religion!"

"No. I'm getting on you for not resolving an important issue in your life. Last winter you began a spiritual quest to find answers to some very important questions. Instead of pushing the matter to a rightful conclusion, you got lazy and let go of it. What kind of writer do you think you will be if you are bored with the most important questions in life? Or will you be content to write repair manuals for automobiles? And if you are too clever for that, then you can write speeches for politicians, too lazy to prepare their own words."

"That's not fair. I read more and study harder than anybody I know. I missed ten years of school, and in one year, I am caught up with my classmates. How dare you call me lazy."

"But, you could do a lot more, if you didn't spend so much time driving up and down Main Street with your friends and drinking beer."

"What's wrong with having a little fun?"

"Since when is it fun to drink yourself sense-less?"

"Guess who taught me that we do not live under the thumb of a God, who dishes out rewards and punishments?"

"You are right. We do not live in a world of rewards and punishments, but we do live in a world of consequences. Staying out late to drink with the boys, reaps bitter fruit. You can put that in the bank."

"Why do I feel like you and Ella are ganging up on me?"

"Because we are. We don't like what is happening to you. When you told her you were going to the mountains and wouldn't see her all summer, why didn't she try to talk you out of it? Why isn't she here today to say good-by to you?"

"She was busy," Danny said, his voice more soft, uncomfortable.

"Too busy. Can't you see you are losing her?"

"There are lots of girls."

"There is only one Ella Cowley. Of all the

people in Cache Valley, why do you suppose she was the only one who could find the lost girl?"

"You can't answer that anymore than I can."

"No, but I can tell you why she is not here with us, today."

"Why?"

"There are lots of other boys."

"What is that supposed to mean?"

"The world is full of people whose main ambition in life is to make money so they can afford to be lazy and comfortable. When you came out of the mountains, I thought you were better than that, something special, maybe a budding young atheist, perhaps something else. Then, after the prom disaster, I thought you might become a fine Christian. I never dreamed you had it in you to be one of those dime-a-dozen lukewarm people who just coast up and down Main Street because some boys told you it was fun. Had I known this was going to happen, I would have sent you back to the mountains."

"At least, I am not a bitter, old man, wasting my life crying over something that wasn't my fault," Danny shot back, hoping his words hurt, too.

"I suppose I deserve that," the professor said, calmly. "Just remember, my Emma was taken from me. You are throwing your Ella away. My seeds of bitterness don't compare to the ones that will someday haunt you. So, have a good summer." Wearily, the professor climbed into the idling automobile and headed back to Logan.

Chapter 20

Danny wasn't very happy as he hiked along the trail, leading to the base of Temple Peak. The professor's words had cut deeply, just when Danny thought his life was moving in the right direction. How could a few words from an old man, turn so many things upside down?

Danny's plan was to set up camp at the den, then find Ephraim. Maybe, they could kill a few sheep together. The thought of fresh lamb made his mouth water.

The continuing sting of the professor's words made Danny want to stay in the mountains, maybe for the remainder of his life. Perhaps, he could find a newspaper or magazine that would buy articles about living in the wilderness. The money would buy enough supplies to enable him to stay in the mountains on a permanent basis. He wouldn't need much. The professor and Ella would never see him again. They could read his articles, if they wished, but that was all.

After three or four miles, Danny heard bells on grazing animals. Then, he heard the bleating of sheep. Then, he saw a white tent nestled under some big pine trees next to a spring. A herder was unsaddling a bay horse. Three dogs were waiting for him to finish.

When the herder turned to place the saddle over a log, Danny recognized the face. It was Frank Clark. Danny's first thought was to avoid the camp, just to sneak by, but then he thought it might not hurt to find out what old Frank was up to.

"Killed any bears, lately?" Danny asked, as he walked into the camp.

"If it ain't the bear-loving kid who writes all them nasty articles," Clark said, grinning from ear to ear. Danny was surprised that Clark recognized him.

"So, have you killed any bears?" Danny repeated his question.

"Not your Old Ephraim. Got me a couple of blacks, but Old Eph is too smart. Maybe, you can tell me how he got so trap savvy."

"I helped him out of a trap, once. He lost a couple of toes. He didn't forget."

"The other day, he pulled a trap out of a waller without even setting it off. Never seen a bear with a soft touch like that before."

"If you'd lost a couple of toes, you'd have a soft touch, too," Danny said, then changed the subject. "They say you killed a hundred bears."

"Fifty three, to be exact, but people likes to round it off to a hundred."

"Will you get him?" Danny asked, his eyes narrowing. "Ephraim's a pretty smart bear."

"He's not very smart, at all," Clark said, his eyes narrowing, too.

"If the bear's not smart, then what does that make you, the man who can't catch him?"

"A smart bear would carry off a lamb, once in a while, when he got hungry, not just wade into a herd, breaking necks and backs and legs, and slinging guts all over the place. Killed six, night before last."

"Maybe, he's trying to tell you to go home, that you are not welcome here. He doesn't think you are getting the message, so he kills more sheep."

"A smart bear wouldn't go back to a waller where Frank Clark hid a trap, a week ago. Three times he pulled my trap out of the same waller up at Spawn Hollow. Would you wade into a wallow where Frank Clark had attempted to trap you on three different occasions?"

"No, I wouldn't," Danny had to confess.

"When the weather gets hot, he'll be in a waller every afternoon. And my 23-pounder will be set and ready every day the rest of this summer. One day, Old Eph will get careless. He only has to make one mistake, then it'll all be over."

Danny had no response. He knew Ephraim was courting disaster.

"Where are you headed?" Frank asked.

"Hoping to find Old Eph, and teach him how to move and set traps, so the next time he finds your 23-pounder, he'll be able to hide it next to your fire, or behind your wagon, and then catch you in it."

"If your livelihood depended on a herd of sheep, you wouldn't be taking sides with no bear."

"That's for sure," Danny agreed, suddenly very tired of discussions that didn't go anywhere.

"What's for supper?" Danny asked.

"No fresh lamb, like what the bear would serve up," Clark responded. "But I got plenty of mutton stew. Made it myself, and it's plenty tasty if you want some."

Danny stayed for supper. The mutton was surprisingly good, but, still, he preferred the fresh, raw lamb which he hoped would become his regular fare in a day or two. By the time they finished eating, it was dark.

When Danny got up to leave, thanking Frank for the meal, the herder seemed surprised that Danny was leaving.

"This is grizzly country, cougars, too," Clark warned. "A man would be crazy, traveling at night without a gun. You're welcome to stay here until morning."

"No thanks. There's enough moonlight to see where I am going," Danny responded.

"You're not afraid?" the herder asked.

"Going to sleep in the presence of a man who killed fifty-three bears, frightens me a lot more than wandering through the woods where a few bears might be feeding."

Clark began to laugh, softly at first, then louder. He found it very funny that this young man was more afraid of a friendly herder than a wild grizzly. He continued to laugh as Danny picked up his pack and headed out.

An hour later, when Danny left the main trail to work his way up to the den, he was careful not to leave any tracks for Clark to follow.

The den was the same as when he, Ella, and Molly had left it the previous winter—except Ephraim was gone, and there was no sign to indicate the bear had been around, recently. Still, Danny unpacked his things, figuring eventually, Ephraim would show up. He knew Ephraim might travel twenty or thirty miles in a single night, so it would be fruitless to try to run him down.

Danny had brought a number of books with him, including the Bible, but the usual passion for reading and learning wasn't there. He spent a lot of time thinking about the things the professor had said, wondering about Ella and why things were changing.

He worried about Ephraim. Eventually Frank Clark would catch him and kill him. A man had a right to protect his sheep. Ephraim had no business killing half a dozen sheep for a single feeding. How do you stop a bear from doing something like that?

Sometimes in the evening, Danny would go down to the beaver ponds and catch a few fish for his supper. It always felt good to be moving about with something to do.

He had been in the mountains over a week, and was just finishing cooking four fish over an open fire, when he looked up and saw Ephraim staring at him at the edge of the fire's light.

When Ephraim growled, Danny tossed him one of the fish. The bear continued to stare at Danny, who looked back at him, surprised at how much bigger the bear seemed. Not fatter, because it was still early in the summer, but taller, broader, and stronger. There was dried blood on his front paws and around his mouth, but not his own blood. Apparently, he had enjoyed a fat lamb for supper.

Finally, Ephraim dropped his nose to the ground and licked up the fish. Danny tossed him another.

After the second fish was swallowed, Ephraim finally walked up to Danny. The boy began scratching the bear's ears. For one night, it was like old times. They slept side by side in the den.

About noon the next day, after sniffing through Danny's stuff and finding nothing to get very excited about, Ephraim simply headed off in the brush and was gone. No parting hug, no good by. Danny realized there was no way to talk to Ephraim, no way to warn him about Frank Clark. Danny felt so helpless.

It was nearly two weeks before Ephraim returned. The weather was a lot warmer, now, and the bear's shaggy coat was thick with half-dried mud—an indication he had spent the afternoon at his favorite wallow. Again, the huge beast bedded down beside Danny to sleep, but this time, Ephraim arose in the middle of the night to embark on another of his quests for food.

From his hilltop hiding places, Danny made it a point to follow Frank Clark's movements whenever possible. On several occasions, when he saw Clark carrying the bear trap to a new wallow, Danny followed the herder, careful to keep out of sight. When the herder had returned to his camp, Danny would find the trap and remove it from the mud, placing it on a nearby bank, where Ephraim would be sure to see it. He hoped the bear would eventually sense the danger of hanging out at the wallows, frequented by Clark. Before leaving the wallow, Danny would always wipe away his own footprints, so Clark would think it was the bear who was tampering with his traps.

Every week or two, Danny visited Clark's camp, usually in the evening. Clark always invited him to stay for supper, and the fare was always the same, mutton stew.

"Don't you get tired of eating the same thing, all the time?" Danny asked, one evening.

"Of course. I hate mutton stew, but that old bear of yours keeps leaving dead sheep around and I hate to see all that meat go to waste. When Old Eph eats sheep, I have to eat sheep, too. Every time I cook up a new pot of stew, I am reminded that it's time to go change the trap again. It might take twenty years, but sooner or later, that old bear will make a mistake, and when he does...."

Danny thanked him for the food and disappeared into the night.

It was August when Danny walked out to the highway and caught a ride into town. School wouldn't be starting for a while, but he needed some supplies, and a few more books. The professor wasn't home, but Rita filled his pack with canned meats and fruits, while he gathered up some books from the study.

Before leaving the house, Danny picked up the phone and called Ella. Her mother said she was visiting an aunt in Idaho and wouldn't be home for about a week. Danny caught a ride back up the canyon, getting out at Temple Fork. It was late in the day, so he climbed partway up a steep hillside, and spent the night under a big tree.

In the middle of the night, he was awakened with a start. He listened for a long time, but couldn't hear anything. Still, his heart was pounding, and he didn't know why. He kept telling himself that nothing was wrong. Still, he couldn't go back to sleep. He remembered Ella's dream, and wondered if something like that was happening to him. Maybe something had happened to Ella up in Idaho, or maybe the Professor had had a heart attack. Maybe Ephraim...."

Still unable to sleep, Danny gathered up his things and began hiking up the canyon. Even without a moon, there was enough light from the stars to allow him to find his way.

Eventually, daylight came. Danny walked faster. Then he saw a rider: Frank Clark. Something was wrong. The herder was moving too fast in the early-morning chill, without hat or coat. His .25-.35 rifle was in his hand, instead of in the scabbard.

Upon seeing Danny, Clark dismounted and shoved the rifle into the scabbard. Then he turned to face Danny.

"They can bring in the poison and those government trappers," he said, his voice trembling. "I'll never kill another bear as long as I live. I don't care if they are eating all my sheep, and one is dragging me off with my foot in its mouth. I'll never kill another bear."

"What happened?" Danny asked.

"Sit down, I'll tell you the whole thing," Clark said, pointing to a fallen log. His hand was shaking. Both of them walked over to the log and sat down. Clark's littlest dog, Jenny, curled up at her master's feet.

"It started yesterday. I checked my trap at a waller in Long Hollow. Old Eph had dragged it out of the mud and set it up on the dry ground. I knew from the missing toes in the track, that it was him. The trap was still set.

"I could see where he had churned up a new waller down the draw a bit. He had opened up the berm at the bottom of the first, to let a little extra water down to the new one. That's where I took the trap. I buried it in the mud, then attached the end of the chain to a fallen log. I never attach the chain to a living tree, or anything that can't be dragged. If a bear can't get away, he'll sometimes chew off his foot. But if he drags off a big, old log, attached to the end of the chain, it's easy to track him down and get him."

Danny was feeling sick to his stomach, and wanted to be anywhere but here, but he forced himself to stay and listen.

"Then, I went back to camp, about a mile down the valley. It was a warm, beautiful evening, with lots of stars. I was sleeping pretty good. Then, suddenly, I waked up to the sound of a terrible roar. First, I thought one of my horses was hurt. Sometimes, a horse will make a terrible noise like that.

"I couldn't go back to sleep, so I decided to get

up and see what was the matter. I didn't think the noise was coming from very far away, so I didn't bother to put my pants on, just slipped into my boots. I picked up my rifle, shoved seven steel-ball cartridges into the magazine, and headed up the trail. My little Jenny didn't want to come, so I let her stay in the tent. If I'd thought about it, I'd have known from her fear, that it was a bear and not a horse I had heard.

"The noise had stopped, so I walked quietly along the trail, hoping it would start up again, so I would know where it was coming from. I hadn't gone very far, when the roar sounded again, this time behind me, down in the willows in the bottom of the hollow. Now, I knew it was a bear that was making the noise. From the sound of him moving through the brush, I figured he had got rid of the big log, and just had the trap and chain attached to his foot. I learned later, that he broke off one of his big teeth, breaking the steel ring that held the chain to the log.

"It was too dark to shoot at him, and I didn't dare go back to camp because the trail I was following, went pretty close to the place where I was hearing the noise. So, I sat down in my underwear, shivering like crazy, and waited for light. I could have warmed myself by moving around, but I didn't want him to know I was there, so I just sat and shivered.

"As I thought about it, I realized that when he got caught in the trap, instead of trying to go up the hollow to get away, he was heading straight for my camp. He knew I was the one who had been putting traps in the wallers, and he knew where my camp was at. He was coming to get me.

"When it finally gets light, I can't see him. I know he's down in the willows, because I didn't hear him leave. I'm tired of shivering, so I get up and walk along the trail back to camp, throwing sticks and rocks into the willows, trying to stir him up. My rifle is ready.

"Suddenly, I hear a bunch of thrashing in the brush, and another roar. I look and look, but can't see anything. Finally, I see what looks like a patch of fur. I aim and fire. It's him, alright, but I just grazed him across the shoulder. He's really mad, now. He roars again, and stands up on his hind legs.

"Now, I can see him. I know it's about ten feet from the tip of his nose to his tail. Add a couple more feet for the hind legs, holding him up. His nose is probably twelve feet off the ground, and he weighs as much as a big horse, about eleven hundred pounds.

"The big trap is clamped on his front foot, and the fourteen-foot chain, attached to the trap, is wrapped around his forearm as careful as a man would do it. He's holding the trap above his head like he is going to hit me with it. There's blood all over his paws and face from trying to tear the trap off.

"He sees me, now, and starts walking towards me. He's so close I can smell him, but there's a four-foot bank between us. If he were down on four feet, something like that wouldn't slow him down, but I don't know if he can get up the bank, walking on two feet. I point the rifle at him and fire five more shots.

"That doesn't put him down, but I know he is

hurt bad because red, foamy blood is coming out his mouth. I save my last bullet. He turns away. I think, for a second, that I have taken the fight out of him, that he doesn't want to get me anymore, because he is moving up the draw. But, that's not the case. He knows a place where the trail comes up the bank. He is going to the trail so he can get on my side of the bank and get me. And that's what he does. In a few seconds he is up on the bank with me and coming after me.

"The fight is out of me, now; I decide to run away. But, just as I turn to do that, little Jenny shows up and starts nipping at Old Eph's heels. He turns to get her, giving me a chance to step up close and put the last bullet in the back of his head. Down he goes. He looks at me, as the life seeps out of that huge body."

Danny just sat there, staring into space. Clark was silent for what seemed a very long time. Finally, he continued his story.

"All along, I thought the bear was Old Eph, because he was so big, and because I had seen his track the day before. But, now, I know it's him because I see the missing toes on his front paw.

"I don't know why I feel so bad. This old bear has been eating my sheep for years, and I finally get him. I should be happy. But I feel terrible, empty, and alone, like I done something terrible. Tears are running down my cheeks. I feel like I'm going to die if I don't talk to somebody in the next few minutes.

"I vowed, then and there, I would never kill another bear, and I intend to keep that promise.

Maybe, I'll have to sell my sheep and get a job in town."

Clark buried his face in his hands. The dog, Jenny, sat up and licked one of his hands. Without a word, Danny stood up and started up the trail. An hour later, he found Ephraim's body stretched across the trail, a short distance above Clark's camp.

Danny sat on the ground and pulled the mangled front paw, the one with the trap on it, into his lap. Carefully, he removed the heavy trap, and unwound the chain that was still wrapped around Ephraim's forearm. Without resetting the trap, Danny carried it into the thick willows and hid it where he thought no one would ever find and use it, again.

Then, he returned to Ephraim, once again sitting on the ground. For the second time, he pulled the mangled paw into his lap—the same paw that had the missing toes.

"Sorry, old boy, but I guess it doesn't hurt anymore," Danny whispered, as he carefully cut away the remaining three claws. These, he placed in his coat pocket. "I just wanted something to help me remember the good times we shared together."

Danny sat there for the better part of an hour, not saying anymore,-just scratching the little ears, and running his fingers through the thick fur.

Danny knew that, eventually, Clark and other herders would return. Everyone would want to see Old Ephraim. Danny guessed the other herders would be boastful and irreverent. They would probably tease Danny about losing his favorite pet. They would want to remove the hide, and other parts. Danny wanted no part of any of this, so he got to his feet, looked at his old friend for the last time, then headed up the mountain to the lonely den.

Danny stretched out on his back under the big cross and looked up at the puffy clouds. When night came, he stared at the stars. He couldn't sleep, and he ignored the pangs of hunger and thirst.

The next day, Danny left the den. Walking helped him think about something besides the pain in his chest. The pangs of hunger and thirst distracted him, too. He walked and walked and walked.

It was late in the day, when he saw the highway, across a sprawling valley of green grass and wild flowers. Two cars were slowly winding their way up the road, almost to the top of the pass where the road began the descent to Bear Lake.

Where the slope below the edge of the road was steepest, at the bottom of a draw, Danny saw the rusted remains of an old car. He was sure it was the same one that had killed his mother nearly a dozen years earlier. He walked down to the twisted remains.

The black paint had been replaced with red rust. The glass had long since been broken from the window areas. The leather padding from the seats was gone, leaving only a few springs and some twisted steel.

He looked up the hill, wondering where they had found his mother's body. He wondered how his life might have been different if the car had traveled only a few hundred yards further, starting down the road into the Bear Lake valley.

Slowly, Danny turned and started back to the cave, trying to remember how he had made that journey in the middle of the night, when he was only five years old. He found the old trail that led in a southerly direction away from the road, but beyond that, he could only guess.

Hours later, upon reaching the cave, he sat down under the cross and pondered the journey he had just made, and the impossibility of a five-year-old boy making the same journey, in a snowstorm, in the middle of the night, without any guidance or direction. There were too many deep gullies, steep hillsides, easy trails leading in other directions. Impossible as it seemed, it had happened.

For the first time since he could remember, Danny rolled onto his knees and offered a prayer. "God, I don't know if you can hear me. I don't even know if you exist. But I also don't believe a little boy could find his way from that wrecked car, to this cave in a winter storm without someone like you to guide him. I thank you for that, for saving my life, for leading me to this den to be fed and taken care of by a mother bear and her cub. I thank you for that."

"But I would also like to know that this prayer is not foolishness. I read in the Book of Kings that when Elijah prayed, you sent down fire from heaven to prove to him and everyone else that you were God and that you lived. Can't you do something like that for me? I don't need a big fire, like the one that consumed Elijah's sacrifice after he poured water on it, but maybe just a little one, just enough to start this dead tree to burning. Amen."

In the partial moonlight, Danny could see the silhouette of the trees that formed the cross. He looked at the base of the tree, then high up, all the way to the top. He repeated the process several times. There was no fire, not even a little smoke. Danny rolled back onto his knees, his eyes open, looking up to the heavens.

"If the fire is too much to ask, how about a little earthquake—not enough to frighten the people in the valley, just a little one to rattle these rocks. Just enough, so I know you can hear me. And, if that's too much to ask, how about a gust of wind. It's a calm, quiet night. Give me a good gust to get this tree swaying back and forth. Then, I will know, like Ella knows. Please. Amen."

Danny sat back against the tree and waited. His open palms were on the bare ground, so he would be able to feel the slightest tremor. His eyes were focused on the tree, waiting for it to bend. But, no wind came, and the ground didn't shake. He waited all night. Nothing.

A second day came and went, then a third. Finally, in an effort to break out of what seemed to be a stalemate, Danny opened the Bible to the place where he had stopped reading, in chapter 18 of the First Book of Kings, where Elijah had called down fire from heaven:

"Then the fire of the Lord fell and consumed the burnt sacrifice, and the wood, and the stones, and the dust, and licked up the water that was in the trench. And when all the people saw it, they fell on their faces: and they said, The Lord, he is the God; the Lord, he is the God"

Danny had read all this before, but as he continued reading in chapter 19, he found a passage that made him stop and think. Elijah, after calling down fire from heaven, was asking the Lord to take his life:

"...O Lord, take away my life; for I am no better than my fathers." In verse 10, Elijah explained why he wanted to die: "...for the children of Israel have forsaken thy covenant, thrown down thine altars, and slain thy prophets with the sword; and I, even I only, am left; and they seek my life, to take it away."

It didn't make sense. The people had seen the great miracle, the fire from heaven. Still, they turned away from God, and Elijah wanted to die because he was the only one left who still believed.

Danny continued to read. Elijah went up on the mountain. A great wind came, but it said the Lord was not in the wind. Then an earthquake, but the Lord was not in the earthquake. Then a fire, and the Lord was not in the fire.

Danny remembered how he had prayed for fire, an earthquake and wind, too, and he hadn't found the Lord in these things either.

Then he read, "...and after the fire a still small voice."

Danny closed the book. He realized, like Elijah, that he had been looking for God in the wrong places. He had been looking outward for fire, earthquakes and powerful winds, when he should have been looking inward, listening for a still, small voice.

Danny sat quietly, listening harder than he had ever listened before hoping to hear a still, small voice. Nothing. He couldn't remember having heard such a voice before, neither in the mountains, nor in the city.

Then, he remembered the night, Joni had killed her last sheep. He remembered the cold, confused feeling. He hadn't heard any words, that danger was near, but he felt it. And Ephraim had felt it, too. Instead of speaking to their minds with English words that a bear cub could not understand, anyway, perhaps, God had whispered to their hearts with feelings. Maybe, that was the still, small voice discovered by Elijah. It made sense.

Danny remembered the first time he had seen Ella, in the market. Something had touched his heart then, too, not the cold, confused feeling like when Joni was shot, but a warm, calm, wonderful feeling, like everything was right in the world. Like God was touching his heart to tell him something good was going to happen. He hadn't thought about it at the time because he was embarrassed, caught chewing on the raw leg of lamb.

As Danny pondered these things, that same feeling returned. He felt joy swelling in his heart—so much so that he thought his heart might burst. Tears were streaming down his cheeks. Never had he felt so good. The still, small voice was speaking to his heart, again, a confirmation that his thinking was sound.

The sadness he had felt at Ephraim's death was

gone. The still, small voice whispered that Ephraim was in a heavenly meadow, stretched out on lush, green grass, spring lambs running playfully about. The bear's body may have been shot full of holes, but the real Ephraim had found a better place.

Danny pondered these things for another day. Then, all of a sudden, he stood up, brushed off the pine needles, and took a deep drink of cool mountain water. He decided it was about time Ella Cowley had another dream come true, the one about her and Danny Evans tying the knot that would last forever.

"Ella," he said, out loud. "Your wish is my command."

Epilogue

I had barely finished reading the above story, when the old man entered the tent. He was of medium height and build, not as skinny as most men in their nineties. It didn't seem to bother him that I was sitting in front of his laptop, and that Russell was sleeping on his bed.

"You must be the Dan Evans I've been reading about," I said, turning my chair all the way around to get a better look at him. He was well-prepared for the rugged, mountain environment, wearing Gortex boots, wool trousers, a Carhart coat, and a sheepskin cap with flaps that could be tied down over the ears.

There was still plenty of sparkle in his blue eyes. He sat down on one of the wooden boxes. Russell finally woke up, pulling himself to a sitting position.

"Did you like the story?" he asked.

"Very much," I responded. "But I have a few questions."

"Fire away."

"Is this Ella?" I asked, pointing to the photo, taped to the wall of the tent—the pretty woman standing in front of the temple.

"Yes, that's my wife. Her dream came true, you know."

"Then what?"

"We went back east to study journalism. University of Pennsylvania. After graduation, I had various jobs in government. Wrote for the *New York Times,* too. On several occasions, Ella had dreams which guided my career, and on one occasion, saved my life."

"What about Stirling Nibley, the professor?"

"Every time we had a new baby, he came to visit. He never re-married. I think he might have crossed over from his atheist point of view, but in his old age, he frequently expressed his abhorrence for deathbed repentance."

"And Old Ephraim. What happened to his remains?"

"After I left, Clark brought Joe Brown and some other herders back. They skinned him so they could have a nice rug. Then, they covered him with brush and set it on fire. They rebuilt it several times, then buried what was left.

"George Hill, a professor at the college and a local scoutmaster, contacted the Smithsonian Institute in Washington D.C., telling them a huge grizzly had been killed in the Cache Mountains. They said they did not believe it was a grizzly, but if he would send them the skull, and it proved to be a grizzly, they would send him a $25 reward for his troop fund.

"The scouts went up there in October, dug up the grave and removed the head. Hill cleaned it up and sent it to Washington. A while later, he received the $25 reward."

"Where is the grave?" I asked. I wasn't sure he wanted to tell me. People are always wanting to dig up special places like that.

"Up the right hand fork, not far from where Long Hollow and Trail Hollow come together. I'm going over there tomorrow, to celebrate finishing the story. Would you like to come?"

The next day as we were hiking over to the grave, Dan explained that a nice monument had been erected. He said that whenever he came to Utah on vacation, he made it a point to visit Ephraim's grave.

"You know," he explained, "when folks visit graves of loved ones, they take flowers—especially on Memorial Day. I take roses to Ella's grave every year. But when I visit Ephraim's final resting place, I never take flowers. Eph never seemed to notice the flowers, much. I take a shank of lamb or mutton, something I know he'd really like. I hang it in a nearby tree. When I come back, it's always gone. I hope that tells him I still care."

I had another question.

"In the story, you tell how you removed three of his claws and put them in your coat pocket. What happened to them?"

"I gave one to Ella the first day of school, that fall. It hung on a string—kind of an engagement necklace. The professor got the second one, and he wore it around his neck until the day he died. And here's the third one." He opened his coat so we could see the claw hanging around his neck. "Reminds me of an old friend who helped me find what I was looking for."

When we reached the grave site, Danny removed a half-frozen leg of lamb from his day pack, but before hanging it in one of the nearby trees, he removed the paper wrapping and bit off a sizable chunk of the raw flesh for himself.